On Front Porch with Helen

Memories of an Unlikely Friendship

Esther Carls Dodgen

Copyright © 2011 by Esther Carls Dodgen

Published by Carpenter's Son Publishing, Franklin, Tennessee

Published in association with Larry Carpenter of Christian Book Services, LLC
www.christianbookservices.com

Edited by David D. Troutman

Cover and Interior Layout Design: Suzanne Lawing

Printed in the United States of America

978-0-9832846-3-5

Table of Contents

Introduction

Our dear sister, Esther, passed away on September 12, 2010 after a three and a half year battle with lymphoma. She left this manuscript unpublished. Our family decided to see her dream fulfilled and come to life. With much thought and the help of Christian Book Services we honor Esther's memory with her story. Our memories of Esther will linger on through this story of Helen and Esther's lives.

The book cover shows her childhood home where she conversed with family and friends and read many books on the front porch. Many memories took place at this home where she and her siblings grew up. The home is still in the family and is the residence of a nephew, Steve Carls, and his family. The drawing was done by a friend of theirs over 25 years ago. Several changes to the outward structure have been made, but the house is still beautiful and well kept.

Most people who were familiar with Esther, knew her as a remarkable, special lady. This book gives many insights to who Esther was, and how she was molded into that person. We hope you enjoy the story of her time with Helen, a kindred spirit.

This book is dedicated to Esther by her siblings, David, Glen and Ruth.

Prologue

I didn't cry when my mother died.

It's not that I didn't care or that I had negative feelings toward her. It's just that she was old. Old people die.

But I am crying now.

I'm at the funeral of an old lady I've known only a few years, a woman who isn't even related to me—and all sorts of emotions are seeping out of me.

I cry when we sing, "And when I think that God His Son not sparing, Sent Him to die, I scarce can take it in."

I cry when Pastor Barone prays, "Gracious and loving God, we are so blessed to have been able to know Helen and to be able to look forward to that great reunion in heaven…"

I cry when I see the reds, yellows, aquamarines, and whites—flowers laid by the coffin that politely, yet assertively, disperse their perfume throughout the chapel. As I looked at the flowers, I thought of the flowers in her yard. And the flowers in my mother's yard.

When a person lives as long as Helen did, through as much history, through as much life, through as much faith in God, a funeral can be more joyful than sad. I know that as well as anyone. Yet as we all stand around celebrating her life, smiling and even laughing, I feel a pang in my chest. And I cry.

Grief. Grief for Helen—and for the others.

It's strange how sorrow can be a sweet emotion. For so many years I didn't know that. I thought that taking time to mourn was really a weakness, a lack of dependence on God. Reflecting on the past would keep you there, and life was just too busy for that kind of luxury.

I've been busy ever since I was a little girl, growing up on a farm in West Central Illinois. And I was even busier when I went off to college to earn my teachers degree. Soon I was making my living as a teacher's assistant while earning my Masters, graduating from the University of Illinois at Champaign. I taught at a community college until I married a fascinating man named Joe, and then took a job at a high school where he was also teaching. We retired the same year after thirty years in the classroom.

Yet, retirement didn't end my busyness. Even then I kept on working—teaching adult classes and helping Joe on our farm. I operated a successful vase manufacturing business and in my spare time began writing—not to mention various hobbies and enterprises, including teaching Sunday school and vacation Bible school and tutoring a few needy students.

And, of course, I served as caregiver for an old woman in her last years.

It's not that I didn't have the opportunity to slow down. One of those opportunities came several years before my mother died. While I was filling in for the regular caregiver who was off for two weeks, Mom had fallen and broken her hip and was taken to the hospital in Springfield by ambulance. I followed by car because I knew I would be leaving soon; I needed to be back in Missouri for work. I spent three complete days in the hospital with Mom, sleeping on the couch, until my sister and brothers could take over. Then I went back to her house, packed my suitcase, and left for home.

I was dead tired and should have slept before taking off; but I wanted a little time with my husband before going to work. An hour after I left, I noticed I was getting sleepy and planned to stop at the nearest exit. I didn't make it. I fell asleep at the wheel. The car went onto the side of the road, and I woke up and overcorrected. The car went into the median and flipped five times, according to eyewitnesses. I had my seatbelt on and received only a bruise or two, but the car was totaled. *I guess God has more work for me to do*, I thought.

So I went back to work and Mom went to a nursing home to finish recuperating. She never left, and passed away within two years.

No, it wasn't a traumatic experience that slowed me down, that got me to cry. It was ordinary life in the ordinary home of an ordinary woman.

CHAPTER 1
Meeting Helen for the First Time

"Some people come upon you like the rising sun."

Helen's house, 220 East Benton in Carrollton, Missouri, was a sturdy brick bungalow built in the early 1900s for a doctor. I pulled into the driveway and studied the place where I'd agreed to spend my nights for several weeks, caring for its ninety-year-old owner.

Except for the expansive, open porch with white-painted ledges that wrapped the front and side like a welcoming banner, the house might have been lost in the shadows of the apartment building next door that had once been a hospital. The lawn, trim and green, showed signs of tender care. Roses, petunias, lilies, pots of geraniums, and beds of perennials flourished without crowding the yard. Flower boxes filled with blossoms of every color trimmed the porch ledges. Hanging baskets of periwinkles and begonias invited me to sit for a while in one of the many pretty chairs that looked out onto the busy street—but it was almost seven and I was expected inside.

I grabbed my overnight bag and stepped out of the car. I had no idea what adventures awaited me inside.

Actually, it wasn't the search for adventure that brought me here at all. It was guilt. Louise, a colleague from my full-time teaching days, had called a couple of years after my retirement asking if I could help her mother for a few weeks after she got out of the hospital. "You once told me that you would like to care for an elderly person after you retired," Louise had said. "Is that still true?"

Was it still true that I hadn't given any substantive care to my mother during her last years, as my siblings did? I wonder.

"I would be honored to help out," I'd told her. The perfect opportunity for penance. Besides, caring for Helen would not interfere with the morning adult literacy classes I taught or my afternoon writing projects. And Joe could live without me in the evenings for a few weeks. No question there.

"I do need to warn you," Louise had said. "Mother can be kind of hard to get along with. She's stubborn."

"Then we'll make a good pair," I said.

Louise laughed, and the deal was set—but I had my reservations. Just because it seems God is leading you to do something doesn't mean it always feels right. It's not that I couldn't handle cranky people. After all, I had been teaching for thirty years. And I certainly didn't mind serving another person. What was creeping under my skin was trepidation associated with impending death. This woman was ninety years old, recovering from hip replacement surgery, and not likely to live long. I didn't relish the idea of spending my evenings in an atmosphere of demise.

It's the same reason I had left my mother to the care of my sister and brothers during her last years. I had told myself it was because I was so busy and lived so far away; but by the time my retirement came around a year after Mom's death, I was ready to admit that it went deeper than that. After all, we make ourselves busy with the things that matter most to us. When I'd thought about it honestly, I had to admit that not caring for her beyond the basics had more to do with my mother than my schedule.

As I opened the heavy door into a little vestibule, I heard voices and quiet laughter. Louise's cheery voice rang out. "Come in, Esther." She opened an inner door and took my overnight bag.

Ornate oak trim adorned the doorways. The old-fashioned ceilings gave it a spacious feel even though someone had squeezed in a couple of extra easy chairs and a coffee table full of plants near the window, plus a quilt-covered twin bed for me. Two stands held carved antique German clocks. Framed photos stood on almost every flat surface. The house held a faint smell of cabbage and antiseptic, of dust and yellowing memories. It felt like I was in a cracked, wrinkled photograph.

And there was Helen.

The patient soon to be in my charge was sitting in an overstuffed chair under an ornately framed reproduction of Monet's Water Lilies, a colorful afghan hanging over the back of her chair. The seat was placed so that she could look out the window and also see who was coming in the door. Beside the chair sat an aluminum walker and a hassock holding a small stack of papers and a phone book. The telephone was on the lamp table on the other side.

Helen was stooped and frail, unable to hide the fact that she had been on this planet many, many decades. She was wearing a pink floral dress. Her curled grey hair was neatly combed. Her skin was soft and wrinkled. Her hazel eyes took in everything.

Helen looked all of her years, but I was struck not so much by the fact that she was old, but that she appeared vibrant. A radiant energy surrounded her. Not an active energy, kinetic and restless, like children have, but a calm and pure energy. She seemed to transmit an invisible glow.

Stubborn, Louise had said. What she hadn't said was incisive. As Helen sat there in her recovery room, supposedly out of commission, she was actively sizing me up. She looked at my face, through the façade of cheerful confidence I had carefully donned, and into the stuff that made me who I was.

I had no place to hide.

Louise began the introductions, but we didn't need them. We already knew the other's name and role; everything else we would have to figure out on our own. Neither of us spoke. We were like two boys circling each other on the playground, each looking for a chance to lay the first punch. We were like magicians, looking for the secrets to each other's tricks.

"Here, Mother," Louise said, probably feeling awkward, "let me straighten your afghan—"

Helen laughed, not unkindly—"Don't fuss over me."—and Louise sat down. Helen smoothed the skirt of her dress and then calmly folded her hands.

I remained standing, considering the mother-daughter duo, but the moment had passed and I soon took my seat beside Louise on the couch across from my host.

"You have quite the green thumb," I said, crossing my legs and wondering what to do with my hands. "I was tempted to take a seat on your porch and enjoy the flowers."

"Tomorrow night we can sit out there if you like."

"I'd like that," I said. "It looks wonderful. You must have been in your garden up until the day you had surgery." I winked. "Either that, or pixies have been at work."

Helen laughed loudly and I felt proud of my little joke.

"Do you garden?" Helen asked.

"I manage to keep a few impatiens and clematis alive." I cringed at my own words, afraid my attempt at modesty had in it a Freudian slip. I sounded as if I expected to have to keep her breathing.

It's not that I had such a fear of death. When you're as convinced as I am that the apostle Paul was right when he said in Philippians, "To live is Christ and to die is gain," the old enemy doesn't scare you much. What scared me was growing old. Lingering.

Why had I accepted this job?

It certainly wasn't money that brought me here.

I wasn't even sure anymore that it was guilt.

No, it was another reason entirely. I could feel it floating in Helen's house now, taking residency, like some faded memory settling down onto the flower print furniture and poking me from behind with thoughts of by-gone days.

Yes, something else…

Helen saved me from my own thoughts. "Gardening must be difficult with everything else you do. Louise tells me you teach classes for students who have not yet completed their high school education."

I happily digressed into a discussion on my tasks—safe territory. I described how the classroom was organized like a study hall with students coming and going at various times, most having different assignments according to their level. "In a way, I'm a private tutor, but I also pair up students to help each other."

"Like you and me," Helen said as she straightened up a pile of papers and a cookbook on her hassock. "Maybe we can teach each other a thing or two."

I smiled charitably. I didn't know I had anything to learn. Andy Rooney once said that "the best classroom in the world is at the feet of an elderly person," but I still placed a higher value on the type of classroom I ran.

The clocks chimed eight o'clock, and Louise stood up. "Mother, let me show Esther a few things before I go."

"Fine. But leave the kitchen to me. I'll show her around in there myself." Helen gave me a saucy wink as Louise and I walked out of the room with Louise gushing about her mother's cooking.

Louise described Helen's needs and then handed me a sheet of instructions. "You don't need to do any housework, of course. The housekeeper will do that."

"That's fine," I said, still reading.

"The housekeeper calls Mother 'Mrs. Chair,'" Louise said nervously, gesturing to all the furniture. "Mother is always inviting folks in, so there is plenty of seating." I nodded and Louise fidgeted, picking up her mother's antique figurines and putting them back down again. "There's not much to do," Louise continued. "Just keep an eye on her when she gets up. Ask her what she wants you to do. Do whatever you see needs done."

"Nothing here I can't handle," I told Louise, aware of her discomfort. "Your mother seems sharp. I'm sure she'll set me straight on anything I forget."

Louise sighed. Her face looked haggard. "This is hard on her. She's so independent."

My mother, like Helen, had been highly independent all her life and needed care toward the end of her life, too. When Mom had been told that there wasn't much of her life left, she'd taken it calmly. She'd even acted upbeat about it.

"We'll be okay," I said. "She'll soon think of me as a companion, not a nurse. And you can stop worrying."

Louise hugged me, a tear in her eye. "Thank you for understanding."

I smiled, believing I knew exactly what she was feeling. I smile now, knowing how little I understood then. When the apostle Paul talked about looking through a glass darkly, I guess he meant that life's lessons can be obscure and hard to figure out. But sometimes we're too immature to even know that our glasses are tinted. Oh, I was no youngster that day I first met Helen. My energy level may not have been what it once was and I might have had a little rheumatism or arthritis by then—but I didn't feel much different than I had ten or even twenty years before.

And I didn't act much differently either.

CHAPTER 2
Getting to Know Helen

Helen planted more than flowers.

After Louise left, I found Helen sewing, threading a needle as nimbly as any young person. Her eyes were still sharp, just like her mind. I fingered the beautiful patchwork quilt on the single bed where I was to sleep. The bed was on the opposite side of the room from the sitting area. From my bed I would be able to see into Helen's bedroom and look in from time to time to see that all was okay.

"Did you make this quilt?" I asked.

"Oh, yes, but that was a long time ago."

"You have so many interests," I commented as I lightly touched the leaves of her African violets. "Cooking, sewing, gardening..."

"That all comes from being a farm wife," Helen said. She and her husband had been diversified farmers—corn, oats, wheat, hay, hogs, cattle, sheep, chickens, and ducks. "It wasn't always easy, but it made me who I am today," she said. "Some people are workers and some are loafers. It seems to follow them all through their lives. My father told me it was better to be in the first group. There was less competition."

"Sounds like something my dad would say," I said, as I continued looking around the room at her plants and knickknacks. "God provides the rain but it is we who till the soil."

"I sometimes think that children are better off when they grow up under somewhat adverse conditions. They need to get used to it early in the game or they won't make it when life gets tough later on."

"Exactly," Helen said, and I was glad to see her nodding approvingly. "People are just like plants. Those that endure some adverse conditions fare better in the end. The tender, hotbed plants die off the first time they get too much sun or water."

"But even plants do better when a skilled hand tends them," I added, admiring the deep green of her Christmas cactus.

Helen nodded with enthusiasm. "Oh, yes. A beautiful garden or a field of grain will respond according to the work put into it. Did you ever try to raise a crop of sweet corn and not expect to till it to keep the weeds from growing?"

I laughed. "I know from experience that if you allow crabgrass to grow with your melon crop, you will not have sweet cantaloupes."

Helen laughed and gestured for me to sit down. "Tell me about your life," she said. "I hear it's been interesting."

"I'm afraid you've been misled," I said as I settled in across from her. "My life has been rather boring."

"You were a teacher, right?" she asked.

"Yes, I taught French in Illinois for seven years, then following my marriage, twenty-three years teaching French, German, and language arts at the local high school."

"Languages! How did you ever learn them?" Helen asked.

"I lived overseas so I could be immersed in the languages."

"Oh my! You were brave. Which countries?"

"Well, first France. I moved to Paris for nine months between my junior and senior year in college, living with a French family." I sank back in the seat, remembering. "I went to school two hours a day to study the language before catching a subway, then a bus to work—and got home late at night."

"Wasn't that dangerous in a big city?" Helen worked nimbly on her sewing, but often looked up to catch my eyes.

"I suppose it was, but I was young and never gave it a thought."

"What work did you do?"

"Food service. I worked at Orly Airport in Paris, which I think is the largest airport in Europe. There were six restaurants of various types, all the way from a snack bar to a five-star restaurant." I could still see the place in my mind's eye. Everything spotless. Shiny floors. Oh, but the people—how friendly and impressed that I had come all the way from America to learn their language and culture. "I usually worked in the *garde manger* which was the main kitchen for all the restaurants. It was where the meat was cut, sandwiches were made, and other specialties such as *canapés* and *croque monsieurs* were created."

"So you were a cook?"

"I did whatever was needed—washed dishes, made sandwiches, delivered items to various restaurants. I also worked for the family I lived with—one hour a day doing the morning dishes and cleaning a room belonging to a boarder."

"Oh my!" Helen looked positively delighted by my story and even forgot about her sewing for a bit.

I kept going. "Then I stayed two months with a German family in Koblenz, Germany. After that I traveled two months around Europe on a Eurailpass while staying at youth hostels."

"How fun! I thought you said your life was boring."

"Fun?" I was surprised to hear it described that way. I was remembering all the work. "Well, I suppose so, but my purpose was serious. I went to learn different cultures and languages so I would make an excellent language teacher."

Helen raised her left eyebrow, a gesture I soon came to love and hate. It indicated she had an opinion that she was keeping to herself. "You learned the language, but what did you learn of the culture?" she asked. "Did you learn how to make *spaetzel*, for example?"

"The German drop noodles?" I shook my head.

She wrinkled her nose. "Too bad," she said. "Cookbooks have the recipe, but you need a private tutor to learn how to make real *spaetzel*. Some night we'll have a go at it. What cookbooks do you use?"

I mentioned my trusty Betty Crocker Cookbook and a recipe collection my church women's group had assembled.

"Oh, the old, historic church on Main Street! Isn't that where—oh, what's her name? The seamstress?" Helen and I began uncovering our mutual friends. Carrollton, Missouri has only a few thousand residents, and Helen seemed to know them all. I felt like I was chatting with a member of my own family. Soon I was describing to her my husband's Angus cattle operation, the Sunday school class I teach, and my extended family. It was fun to talk about my family history with someone who was clearly so interested.

I continued telling Helen the story of my family. My father's mother, Victoria Elizabeth, had pneumonia and was in bed off and on several years before her death at age twenty-nine on February 2, 1914. William, my father's older brother, remembers taking the streetcar to St. John's Hospital in Springfield, Illinois to visit their mother sometimes in the evening. She was in the hospital for months. The railroad was close-by and the engine bell would 'ding-a-ling' all the time they were there. He has never liked to hear a train bell since then. After they returned home, their father would take a drink of cheap corn whiskey before going to bed.

William, in actuality, became head of the household at age five and remembers preparing a gourmet dinner one day for their ailing mother in bed. He fried some sliced potatoes in a skillet, adding some water to keep them from burning. He recollected, "I do not think they were very good, but she ate them since her Willie fried them." The children all referred to their mother as their 'angel' mother.

The family lived in a three-room house, 'hovel' as William called it, at 1526 S. Walnut Street in Springfield. They were terribly poor, having no heat except a cook stove and a coal burning heating stove.

My father Arthur coped magnificently with his own limitations, but couldn't entirely overcome his childhood issues. He had been an unwanted orphan at age six after the death of his mother, and was rejected by his drunken father who abandoned his four children after that tragedy. Their mother was buried in Oak Ridge Cemetery in Springfield, an eighth of a mile from Abraham Lincoln's tomb. William, who was eight, vividly remembers it was a beautiful February morning when their father dropped him and my father off at one orphanage and the two younger children, James, 4, and Mary, 2, at another orphanage in Springfield.

Living in an orphanage left many scars on my father. His most vivid memories were wearing hand-me-down shoes that were too small and eating beans and cornbread while the workers had fried chicken. He later went to a foster home where he was severely mistreated. Years later his hands still burned in his memory from having them put on a hot stove. He remembered picking up coal along the railroad tracks as fuel for the stove.

Their father James Russell Dunaway later went back to the home where he had taken his children and was told that the papers he signed gave them up for adoption, and he could not see them anymore. It was unfortunate that the children never knew that their father had come back to see them. They thought he had abandoned them and learned the truth only years later. Since their father had no hope of seeing his children again, he moved to Canada, joined the Army, and eventually remarried and had another child.

The woman in charge of the home for orphans and unwed mothers was interested in putting children out for adoption and had no concern about keeping families together. Actually, she made more money by individual adoptions. In 1914 there were almost no state regulations for such homes. At age six, my father felt devastated, without a friend in the world. He desperately needed to know that someone was watching out for him, to know there was someone who would not leave, someone who would make him feel he mattered. He needed a loving home, as any kid does. When my father was taken from the foster home, the State notified the Carls family, who had already adopted his older brother William three years earlier from an orphanage in White Hall.

William recalls telling his new family he would love to have his brother Arthur come and move in with the family. Was it just a coincidence these two events happened at the same time—William's request and the State contacting the family? Anyway, it soon came to pass that Arthur arrived late one evening at the Carls family home in rural Cass County, Illinois. My dad recalled years later, "I was so happy to meet Bill, but it was the next morning at daybreak that I became overwhelmed with joy. I heard the guineas calling, looked out the window, and recognized the Promised Land. It felt as if I had entered the land which flowed with milk and honey!"

I took a break from my story and watered Helen's flowers. When I started helping her sort through some old newspaper clippings, I continued my story.

Unfortunately, for my father, Cass County was not exactly the land of milk and honey. He was glad to be adopted, but he always secretly felt he was there mainly to help with the farm work. William laughingly recalled years later that they had "shoved a lot of the hard work onto unsuspecting Arthur." William recalls having to plow a 30 acre field with a horse-drawn plow at age nine.

Hard work and strong discipline. That's all my dad knew. In spite of the hard work, the brothers remembered thinking that the family was lazy, not true farmers. No wonder he worked so hard making life better for his family. But he knew he existed and he knew God had a plan for his life, even though he didn't learn that in the home. Hasn't God implanted in all of us a sense of eternity?

In 1923 the boys' adoptive mother Eva died from pneumonia at age thirty-one, leaving their father Julius and Eva's mother Rose to care for the boys. She continued the strict discipline the boys had become accustomed to in the orphanage. Grandma Rose was grief stricken by the death of her daughter and some believe her broken-heart eventually contributed to her death in 1935. How could she give her attention to two young, struggling boys when her heart was so full of grief for her daughter?

My dad discovered later when he applied for Social Security that no adoption papers were ever filed. Probably another blow to his ego! Since he wasn't a legal son, no inheritance from his so called adoptive father was understood, but not unconceivable. A couple of dollars, a watch, or even a letter would have been nice. No papers, no mementos, no photos, no love. The only joy was Brother William.

In spite of that joy, in my father's mind, William was the favored son.

"What a burden to grow up with that feeling," Helen said. It was getting dark and the mosquitoes seemed to enjoy our company too much, but Helen urged me to continue.

William and Arthur's relationship with each other was not affected, though. They remained close throughout life, helped each other on their farms, and did many of the same things. They both raised cantaloupes, had produce markets, sold Christmas trees, and farmed in Florida in the winter. They loved playing horseshoes together and could definitely talk up a storm. All of us cousins still recall the many happy days we played and laughed together—putting on plays from nursery rhymes, playing monopoly and swinging on a sack swing tied to a high branch.

It was not until thirty-six years after their mother Victoria's death that Arthur and William again saw their brother, James, and sister, Mary. There was an inheritance to distribute. Their grandmother Baker, Victoria's mother, had died in a nursing home fire, leaving each of them $7.85.

"And they were finally reunited," Helen said. "How sad, yet at the same time, how uplifting.'

Yes, out of the bad came the good. The two brothers were determined to overcome, and they did.

Helen's advice would be the same as William's and Arthur's: "When things go wrong, get over it and move on. Do you want to live in the past, or do you want to live now? It is not what happens to a person that counts, but what a person learns from what happens to him or her and what they do with what they learn."

Helen turned her head to gaze out the window at her garden. The sun had nearly sunk, and the last rays were reflecting off the pink roses. "Were your grandparents nearby?"

Helen didn't ask a thing about children, and I yapped happily on. My grandmother Mathilda had been my hero.

Before I knew it, the clock chimed ten o'clock. I glanced at the photograph of Helen and her family in front of the philodendron and realized I'd forgotten to ask her about them. She had managed to get me to do all the talking, and I hadn't even noticed.

Helen yawned and stretched. "Time for this old woman to hit the hay. Takes a bit longer to get ready these days, like being a baby all over again."

She made moves to get up from her easy chair with the aid of her walker, and I quickly stood to help. Helen's house was divided into two apartments. Helen's side had once been a doctor's home and office; the side which she rented out had been the waiting room and examination area. Helen's side was similar to a shotgun house—one room went straight into another. In front was the living room, followed by the bedroom, the dining room, and the kitchen. A short hallway separating the bedroom from the dining room had a door to a small bathroom.

We made it from the living room into the next room, the bedroom, without mishap. Helen insisted on doing as much on her own as she could, but I helped her into her nightgown, brushed her hair, and fussed with her pillows and comforter.

"I guess each one of us needs help at some point," she said as she allowed me to assist her into bed.

I smiled. I had been accepted.

By the time she fell asleep it was nearly eleven o'clock. I pulled a book from my bag and tried to read for a bit, but my mind stayed fixed on the woman I had just met. Helen was clearly content to chat the evening away with a stranger whose very presence testified to her loss of independence. Even from just a few hours together, I could see this woman was strong and self-reliant. Now she had to receive help. But why was she so interesting to me? My mind mulled over the possibilities.

The clocks chimed again. I wouldn't be able to sleep with that racket. Carefully, I opened the doors and stopped the pendulums. I'd have to remember to start them again in the morning.

CHAPTER 3
The Value of Being Willing to Work

God gives birds their food,
but he doesn't throw it into their nests.
GREEK PROVERB

By my second night at Helen's, I felt as much at home there as I did in my own place—which had more to do with Helen's hospitality than my adaptability. I easily found my way around and helped wherever I could. The laundry room was to the side of the kitchen before the back porch. I did the laundry and helped straighten up the kitchen.

I also better knew how to resist Helen's smooth self-deflection, and remembered to ask as much about her as she did about me. It was not that Helen was shy or closed; and she certainly wasn't prying for information from me. She simply put others first without even making them aware she was doing it. But this time when I sat down in the charming old house that so closely reflected its owner, I was ready to find out what made this lady tick.

Helen Mary Ann Harper Raasch was born in 1910 when William Howard Taft was president. It was the year that Halley's comet passed the sun without catastrophe. Many believed that the earth would pass through the comet's tail and be destroyed.

Her father, Floyd, was a horse trader as well as a farmer. He suffered from terrible asthma attacks so his wife, Katie, developed her own milk delivery route in nearby DeWitt, a thriving town of four hundred twenty-five people. Helen had been only four when her mother taught her to pack bottles of milk to sell in town.

"I remember my daddy's face when I bragged to him after my first morning on the job," Helen said. She laughed and spoke in a falsetto voice: "'I'm a helper, Daddy. I put the bottles in the crate.' My father didn't miss a beat. He told me what an important part of the farm operation that job was and that I had a right to be proud."

Helen's days began before the sun peeked above the open horizon of the Missouri farm where she was born. With her mother, Helen would sit on the springboard of a two-wheeled cart pulled by their pony as they went from house to house.

I was disappointed when the telephone rang, cutting off the story. I loved the image of Helen and her mother working together.

Helen's daughter Lillie was calling to check in. Helen was clearly pleased, but brushed off queries about her health.

I stood up and found a dusting cloth. I wasn't one to sit around. And there was plenty to do; Helen had a host of knick-knacks and picture frames—photos mostly of what appeared to be family and some of Helen on trips around the United States with her friends. One picture showed a group of ladies in front of a spacious garden of tulips at the Amana Colonies in Iowa.

Yes, Helen was full of surprises.

And she surprised me in ways I'd never expected.

Like her sense of humor.

"When will you be dropping off all those pecans to be shelled?" Helen said into the phone. She paused to listen to her daughter's answer—undoubtedly protestations about putting Helen to work—and then said, "It was my hip the doctors replaced, dear, not my hands." She winked at me.

When she hung up, Helen played the curmudgeon, but she couldn't hide the pleasure she took in her daughter. "Lillie Lou gets a good two hundred pounds of pecans from the tree in her back yard each year. There's no reason I can't still separate out the shells."

"Plus it will give you something to do," I said. I saw the value in that.

"Really!" Helen agreed, eyeing me approvingly as I worked. "What does she think I'm going to do all day? The kids think a television would help 'occupy my time.' Waste my time is more like it. As if a little operation would make me want to spend the day watching TV."

I looked around the room. "You don't own a television, do you?"

She chuckled. "No. The neighbors think it's because I'm cheap. But, I tell you, I've seen enough that I won't have one in my house. Once I caught a glimpse of *The Jerry Springer Show* over at Lucille's. I left disgusted. I'm not sure I'm old enough to understand that kind of entertainment."

I laughed. "You could teach them a thing or two about real entertainment, couldn't you? I'll bet Jerry is laughing all the way to the bank," I said. It felt good to have a meeting of like minds.

Helen laughed too. "Do you think they would go for our brand of excitement?" she asked. "I know Lucille wouldn't." I had met Lucille my first morning at Helen's as I was preparing to leave. She was a cheery woman of about seventy who lived on the other side of the house.

"I think we're going to have fun together. I like the way you think," I said.

Chortling, Helen nodded and picked up her sewing again. Soon her fingers were a blur of motion. After a moment, she paused and raised her head. "You like to keep busy, too, don't you? Still teaching and writing when others are expecting you to sit down and relax."

I nodded, and put the dusting cloth in the laundry basket.

"As my mother always said," Helen continued, 'If you sit down, it's over. Let's get it done first.' I told my children the same thing when they were growing up."

I wanted to cheer. Instead I picked up an afghan and began refolding it.

"I admired my mother," Helen continued, almost finished with her embroidery. "She was a little Dutch firebrand."

"Dutch? Is that your heritage?"

"You know, as in Pennsylvania Dutch," she said. I did know. My grandparents used to talk about being Dutch. It came from the German word "Deutsch," meaning German. The Germans were often called Dutch.

"So, you're German, like me," I said.

"Yes, my grandparents sailed to America from the Alsace area of Germany. Times were tough in the old country. What did they have to lose? They packed their bags and never looked back."

She could have been reciting my own family history. My great-great-great-great grandparents along with their children and grandchildren immigrated to America in pursuit of a better life. As a child, I was told tales of Napoleon and his armies rolling through the streets of my ancestors' hometown in Saxony. Wanting to keep their grandsons from being conscripted into the Army, they set sail on November 10, 1834, arriving in New Orleans seven weeks later. There was a surge of German immigrants into America around that time. About four million Germans came between the 1840s and the 1880s, mainly because of the political turmoil sweeping through Central Europe.

But I was interested in the Dutch firebrand. "Is your mother the reason you're such a hard worker?"

"Believe it," Helen said. "I imitated her, and she imitated her mother, Mary, who imitated her mother, May. Our family knew nothing else." It was quite evident to me that Helen came from a long line of strong women. When Helen married, she did everything her husband did on the farm, as her mother and grandmother had before her: milked, butchered, patched fences, and pitched in with all the rest of the chores. The family raised chickens and cows, and they traded eggs and cream for flour and sugar and a few other staples at the neighborhood store in DeWitt. Most of the rest of their food came from their own fields. Wild game and wild blackberries were an added treat.

"How did you find time for housework and taking care of the children?" I asked. I don't know what prompted me to ask. It's not that children ever prevented me from doing my work. Perhaps it was that my admiration for Helen was growing, and I was caught up in her story rather than my own.

"In those days we didn't work from nine to five. The day started with the rising of the sun and ended when the day's work was done. Even the children pitched in. They were with us and we talked and played while we worked." This reminded Helen of an afternoon harrowing a five-acre field with her two mules, Mike and Beck. She set five-year-old Louise beside her on the springboard and gave her the reins. "Of course, we looked like dirt from all the dust when we finished, but it was a great lesson for Louise. She learned the pride of working."

"I'll bet you looked like the French painting 'A Helping Hand,'" I said.

"I don't think I know that one."

"An old man is seated in a boat with his little granddaughter at his side."

Helen's eyes lit up. "I do know it. Both are holding an oar. She looks like she thinks she's helping him, but he's doing all the work."

"Yup. That's the one," I said. "It's by Emile Renouf." I used to stare at that picture for hours, imagining myself to be the little girl. Even when I was old enough to understand that the little girl wasn't really helping, I still loved the picture.

I headed over to a bookshelf and started straightening the books. "Louise might not have been helping you at first," I said, "but my guess is that she soon was. I know for myself what a hard worker she is." She has a way with the kids she helps at school.

"That's right. Not a lazybones in our house," Helen said. "There couldn't be. We always had plenty to do on a farm. Even though machinery broke down and the weather didn't always cooperate, we took the advice in Ecclesiastes: 'If you wait for perfect conditions, you will never get anything done.'"

Helen told me how Lillie, her oldest, took two jugs of water at a time on their pony to the men in the fields during harvest. Louise milked cows and fed livestock. Thelma, her middle daughter who now lives in Branson, had to clean the cream separator every day. Her son Harold, who lives near Kansas City, hauled the milk and eggs to town in a trailer behind their '35 Chevy. They all helped with group events like butchering, digging potatoes, and gathering eggs.

If only my own mother had treated me the way Helen did her kids. I thought back to those early years I had tried so hard to please my parents. Perhaps this longing stemmed from a poem by Emily Dickinson that I had memorized as a fifth grader.

They might not need me—yet they might;

I'll let my heart be just in sight.

A smile so small as mine might be

Precisely their necessity.

But Mom simply wouldn't let me prove my worth.

"Esther, I want you to rake the alfalfa on the South 20 today," my father would say. "It's ready. Homer will be here at 3:30 to bale it."

Before I would get a chance to ask, "When do I start?" my mother would calmly say, "I have things for her to do around the house"—firmly sparing me again from some of the more difficult farm work my father would have me do.

"My mother was so different from you," I said to Helen. "She'd be telling both of us to sit down and relax. She hated it that I was always such a workaholic."

"You think of yourself as a workaholic?"

"Well, that's what people say." I came back to the couch and sat down again. "I really don't see it as a bad thing, though. My husband and I both work hard, and it's nice to have that in common. Besides, work is a part of the fabric of American life here in the Midwest, don't you think?"

"Yes, it is," Helen said. "That's why I figured you came from a hard-working family."

"Oh, don't get me wrong. My mother was certainly a hard worker. She was the oldest of ten children (two others had died in infancy), and the youngest pretty much became her responsibility. She certainly knew what hard labor meant."

My parents married in 1934 and rented a small farm where they grew some cantaloupes and then bought an 80 acre farm four years later and raised melons and a few years later they added sweet potatoes to their enterprise, stored them in their heated basement and sold them all winter long. In the winter Dad cut mine props from trees on the place, split the trees into posts and hauled them to Springfield to use in coal mines. He'd come back with a load of coal which he sold to local farmers."

"Very smart," Helen said.

"Yes, my dad was innovative."

"In 1942, my parents were able to buy a one-hundred-and-sixty acre farm for twenty dollars an acre," I said. "Dad cut the posts from the Osage orange trees in the hedge rows on the land. The trees had been planted years earlier to prevent the soil from eroding. But my dad knew how to cultivate the land to keep it from blowing. About this time they increased their acreage of cantaloupes and watermelons to one hundred acres. They paid off the farm in a couple of years from the hedge posts and melons. "

"How did they manage all the work?"

"They had help, of course. Dad hired a fellow named Jake Buck who did a super job of finding good workers. Lots of people were out of work in the early 40's and needing a job. Jake would round them up in town each morning and bring them out to the farm to hoe or pick melons. Dad would be up at the crack of dawn to make the rounds in Springfield to sell the produce to stores. Later on, he would have tractor trailers come in and haul them off to Chicago or St. Louis."

"Raising cantaloupes is labor intensive," Helen said.

"Yes, but it pays off financially if one is not afraid of work, and my family was definitely not afraid of work."

I told Helen how my parents once raised six acres of turnips and got the local FFA chapter involved. "The kids dug the turnips and cut off the tops to raise money for the school."

Helen nodded. "One person's enterprise creates jobs for others."

"Later on when we kids were old enough, we pitched right in and had a lot of fun packing crates of cantaloupes with 6, 8, 10, 12 to a crate, depending on the size. Sometimes I picked, sometimes I drove the tractor pulling the wagon for the picking crew. That was the easiest job. But packing the crates under the big mulberry shade trees was not bad. Earlier in the season, we all hoed the melon plants as they were growing."

"That's a big undertaking."

"It was. And that wasn't all. When Dad raised twenty acres of sweet corn, he'd take a lot of corn to larger towns around, including Decatur and Peoria, and later got Schnitker Truck Lines to haul corn in their semis to Chicago. My brother, Dave, says that first year he had early corn before anyone else, and sold it for three dollars a sack of six dozen ears. People were hungry for it. Later we kids were all involved in picking and sacking sweet corn."

Helen had her eyes closed and a contented look came over her face. When I stopped talking, her eyes popped open. "I love hearing about your father. He's the kind of man who helped make this country great. I'll bet he never sat down before the work was done."

I nodded. "You might think he had enough work around home, but not Dad. He bought a truck farm northeast of Orlando, Florida, and grew vegetables during the winter. We came back to Illinois in time for the spring planting. Apparently the experience was not particularly profitable. His brother Bill, who bought a farm in Florida at the same time, said he came back with fifty cents more than before he started, but he described the whole experience in Florida as "the most fun he ever had." My cousin called it a "thrill.""

"In addition to raising sweet potatoes, cutting trees for mine props, and hauling coal back from the mines, he did a lot of different things through the years to support our family and get ahead.

Sometimes he'd buy a truckload of pecans in Mississippi, pack them in ten pound sacks, and sell them at the auctions in Woodson, Rushville, or Ashland. He had a produce market for a few years. After taking a load of squash, pumpkins, or sweet corn to St. Louis to sell, he'd bring back for his market produce that he did not raise or could not get from local farms. My brother, Dave, remembers going along to Michigan to get apples. Later when we kids were in our teens, Dad earned extra cash several winters by buying truckloads of Christmas trees and selling them at an empty lot in town."

"I'm always amazed by God's blessings," Helen said, "and how hardworking people can always wrest a living from the soil. You sure have an interesting family." She meant it and I smiled inside. I had never before looked upon my family as interesting.

"What a great heritage for you. It seems strange that your mother didn't like for you to work so hard," Helen said. "I wonder why."

For the first time ever I wondered, too. Maybe there was more to the story than I recognized. It was Helen who made me think. Why had I never asked my mother about the work she had to do while growing up and how it made her feel and how it affected her? Why didn't I try to understand? I remember many times sitting with my mother and sister on the benches of our grape vine arbor just outside our back porch door while snipping beans, hulling peas, or cutting corn off the cob. Why didn't I ask her those questions then? I guess as a youngster one is too self-absorbed and narrow-minded to think deeply of others. I realize now that she simply wanted to spare me the hard work she had to endure when she was my age.

While growing up, I remember vividly asking my mother, "What do you want me to do now?" What other child would continually ask her mother that question? Wanting to please her was woven into my innermost being, into the fabric of who I was.

"What was she like?" Helen asked.

"My mother?"

"Yes."

My memories flitted back to a younger version of my mother, around the age of forty-five. She was pretty then—she had a shapely figure and soft hazel eyes. Her dark brown hair, which she kept short and curled, was thick and shiny. She was always dressed neatly and kept good posture. At home she wore colorful dresses with an apron. In the garden she wore a bonnet and had long sleeves to keep her skin soft. Dressed up, she usually wore a decorative pin or corsage which she made. Mom didn't have the poise that some women have, where everyone wants to hear what she has to say; or the magnetism that makes people want to stop and stare. Her careful mix of humility and pride made her rather unnoticeable to others.

"She was … normal," I said.

Helen did the eyebrow thing and went back to her sewing.

My mother was not exactly the most nurturing parent that ever raised a child. Apparently even in childhood she had not been easy to live with. Because of an illness, St. Vitus Dance as they called it, she had missed her eighth grade of school and had to make it up. Her sister Rosa remembers how my mother was unable to do her share of the work for a period of time—perhaps a year—and she, Rosa, had thought it unfair. "I would wonder why she didn't need to help with anything when I did," Rosa once told me. "I just didn't understand back then." I suppose that was Rosa's way of telling me she could identify with what I was going through as I dealt with emotions about my mother.

I thought back to what I knew of my mother's history. She overcame the pronounced effects of her illness in later adulthood and managed to live a basically normal life. But long before I knew of her illness, I knew how I felt about my mother. I felt held at a distance. Alone. Forced to struggle with learning the fundamentals of womanhood on my own. Her fragility and inability to love unconditionally hindered me from gaining the self-confidence I saw in my friends.

Yet, I had come to terms with all this—I thought—and reminded myself often of all the struggles she had overcome.

"What was she like?" Helen had asked. Memories of my mother flooded my thoughts.

"Are you sure that's the one you want," my mother would ask when my sister or I would pick out a dress or purse or shoes. It wasn't that she didn't want us to have them. She just wanted to make sure. We were frugal and she didn't want us to buy things we didn't like and need. I know this is the source of my own indecision today.

Did my mother love me? I think so. Or at least I want to think so. In her own way. I cling to that. I need that. Am I fooling myself? She loved me as much as she was capable of loving anyone.

I remember once when I came home from college for Christmas vacation, someone asked her, "Did you miss Esther?" Her words penetrated to the depths of my heart. "Her father probably did." How that hurt! I realize that now she just didn't know how to express her emotions. I, too, sometimes have trouble with that today.

My mother probably can trace her lack of emotional support back to her own childhood. Her mother didn't have time for her. Being the oldest of ten children (two died very young), my mother had big responsibilities. There was no time for intimacy.

I remember one time when this tendency to be indecisive crept into my life. When my husband and I went to select our furniture for our home when we moved upstairs from the basement, it was not easy for me. He saw immediately what he liked. I liked it too, but I had to think about it. I had to mentally place it in the living room. Where would each piece be best placed? Would it look good with the carpeting, with the woodwork? Would it be inviting and comfortable to guests? I was frustrated because I needed a little time to think about the possibilities. Just as I do today.

I still have a hard time making up my mind. I still ask others' opinions— others—whom I respect and admire. They keep telling me, "It's your book…, It's your home…, It's your money, you make the decision." Of course, I can't, but I try. I know they are right. Perhaps asking others is a substitute for my mother's approval. I recognize the origin of it all. I know why. It's just that I can't seem to change. Maybe it's okay to have a few hang-ups. Life would be easier without them, but I have managed.

If I didn't have this hang-up, maybe I would not have a deep appreciation of beauty and simplicity that my mother gave me. And I wouldn't trade that for anything. I thank God every day for what I have—a deep sense of His presence. Maybe I shouldn't try to change. Maybe it has led me to these greater blessings.

No, my childhood had been quite good. I could see that we had been a cohesive unit that was secure. I had learned self-sufficiency, honesty, how to get along. The only thing missing was closeness; and no family, I reasoned, is perfect.

My mother may have made mistakes, but she had deserved my care. I couldn't go back in time and make things right, but I could learn from my mistakes and give assistance to others. And that's why I was at Helen's now, an atmosphere of demise notwithstanding.

My mind snapped back to the present when Helen interrupted my thoughts about my mother.

"The desire to pitch in must start young," Helen said after a moment of silence, as if reciting a Bible verse. "The folks from the old country knew that. Children must be taught if they want something to happen in life, they must work for it. To climb a ladder you must start at the bottom. If something happens you don't like, deal with it, grow from it, and move on. Don't just wish, complain, or blame."

She was preaching to the choir.

"Even when I moved to town after my husband Awald died," Helen went on, "I still tried to keep up with the farming operation." Helen's eyes were on me, picking up clues of my interest. My eyes were wide open. "I stayed there over a year before I rented out the farm and bought this little duplex. It was a lot of work, but I wouldn't have done it any other way."

"You must have bumped into Colin Powell when he was a boy," I said.

Helen looked at me like I was crazy. "You mean the general who became Secretary of State? I never met the man."

"What I meant was, he must have learned his life lessons from someone like you. I read that he accepted his first job as a porter not knowing what a porter did. He learned the first day when they gave him a mop."

"I bet I can tell you the rest of the story," Helen said. "He did that job so well his efforts were recognized, and he soon got a better job."

I laughed and nodded. "That's exactly right."

"Anyone who does his job well," Helen said, "will not only enjoy satisfaction, but his efforts will be noticed. If you are willing to work, you can generally get along without too much difficulty in this world."

I grasped her hand and gave it a squeeze, stopping her fingers from working for a moment. "Exactly," I said.

She understood. She understood me.

But this is not the only reason I am crying at her funeral.

CHAPTER 4
There is No Better Feeling Than Being Accepted

"A good friend is better than a therapist."
BARBARA JOHNSON

It was a humid August evening, and Helen and I were sitting on her front porch, simply enjoying nature and being together. We could have been in her air-conditioned house, but the outdoors suited us better. Some evenings Helen and I continued our discussion after dark. The peaceful moonlight seemed to elevate our moods.

The front porch was Helen's favorite place to meditate in the summer even when no one was around. She liked the solitude. "It gives me time to think," she often said. She could think while sewing, shelling peas, peeling apples, reading, or doing a thousand other things. Her street was a busy place, but solitude is an inner quality, and she practiced it amidst the hustle and bustle. Sometimes God speaks loudly, but more often He speaks in a still, small voice.

I was savoring our time together, knowing it was my last evening there. Helen's health was improving each day. She had a good support system in Lillie and Louise and good neighbors, like Mary Martha and her husband, Pat. She didn't really need me anymore, though it had been a good experience for both of us. I was her transition into dependent living, and she was my transition into retirement. The transition, though, was ending far too soon, and neither of us was quite ready for the next step.

"I love your trees," I said aloud, and got up to clean out the dry leaves from under her bushes. Two large sweet gum trees proudly stood in Helen's front yard near the street.

"The Street Department wanted to cut them down because of the power lines, but I insisted on keeping them," Helen said from her spot on the porch. "Keeping them trimmed has been a whole lot of work, but it's worth it. Those trees have relaxed and comforted me on many hot summer days."

"Yes, beauty and inspiration are important."

"What is life without those things?"

"You did the right thing by fighting for those trees," I said, nodding, leaning on my rake to admire them. "I think sometimes a thought comes to you so strongly, you sense it is not yours, but must have come directly from God."

Helen smiled and said, "Isn't that being a little uppity, thinking we really know God's will? Sometimes we can misread it, especially if we get caught up in our own desires."

I cringed. "Yes, that's true. We have to be careful. Hatred has been kindled and wars fought all in the misguided notion of knowing God's will. Abortion clinic killings, hatred spewing forth on picket lines, terrorism—all in the name of God."

"Yes." Helen continued as I put the rake down and sat in a rocking chair on the porch. "Even so, I have had moments when something that was there all along became clear."

"I believe the Holy Spirit will help us discern these things."

Our discussions were rarely chit-chat or idle gossip. Some people can talk incessantly about themselves, their family, and their interests; but most people do not want to know the intimate details of others' mundane lives. Helen was interested in a thousand things outside herself. We talked about everything from politics to poetry. When I was with her, I had her undivided attention.

Like the evening Helen was picking out pecans from the cracked shells at the kitchen table and I was reading aloud a brief chapter from *My Pillow Book* by Alice Hegan Rice. It is a short book, printed in 1937, detailing the author's thoughts during a lifetime of seeking the spiritual life. We both agreed it was an A+ book that seemed to have been lying there waiting for us to find.

"Don't you feel some books were meant just for you at particular times in your life?" I asked. "I often get that feeling."

Another time as we rocked away on the porch Helen mentioned the scare the U. S. government put into German-Americans in the 40's.

"What do you mean?" I asked, surprised I hadn't heard about this. I'd heard only of this happening to other nationalities—the Russians, the Italians, the Irish, the Japanese, and even recently the Mexicans.

"Oh yes," she said. "Many Germans, like the Japanese, were forced into internment camps. They were labeled threats to the public safety without ever being told what their charges were; and they were refused legal counsel."

"I do remember my parents talking about hiding their German ancestry during the war." Many changed the spelling of their names to sound more American, like changing the k's to c's or ei's to i's. I later learned that there were fifteen thousand German-Americans sent to internment camps, but none was ever convicted of a war-related crime.

We had many great conversations like this during our three weeks together, but for as much time as I had spent with Helen, I rarely had her to myself. The whole town seemed to be aware of Helen's hospitality. Apparently it had always been that way. Helen's house in the country was the hub on Memorial Day weekend when family and life-long friends stopped by on their way to the cemetery in DeWitt. Friends and neighbors told me that Helen could always come up with a meal at a minute's notice for any number of people who stopped by.

"The big family get-togethers were usually at our house because we had plenty of room for everyone," Helen once said.

"I doubt that was the only reason why everyone liked to come to your house," I replied.

Bonnie, a childhood friend of Helen's daughter Lillie, and now my good friend, told me about going to Lillie's house and playing. She said, "Helen was wonderful. The more kids who came, the better. We had to follow the rules, but we always wanted to come back."

And things had not changed now that Helen lived in town.

By now I was used to people popping in to visit Helen, but tonight I was rather hoping I would have Helen all to myself. So when a plump woman with short straight hair wearing a man's hat came smiling, waving and charging through the back yard poppies and cosmos, I inwardly groaned. As soon as the woman started talking, I groaned even more. She was a fidgety woman who didn't like silence, someone who knew what she wanted and wasn't afraid to say it.

"Well, hello, Pearly," Helen said warmly. She turned to me, "Esther, this is my backyard neighbor. I don't think you've met yet."

"Hello," I said as kindly as I could.

Pearl must not have noticed my hesitancy. "Oh, we're more than backdoor neighbors, Helen," she said, laughing. She turned to me too, as if I were the audience, and held on to my forearm. "Helen and I go way back. We were neighbors when we were girls, growing up in the country." She said it as if that gave her some sort of ownership of Helen.

The longer Pearl stayed, the more aware I became of her lack of social skills. She talked too loud and too much. She talked a lot about herself. But Helen didn't seem to notice any of it. She laughed at Pearl's jokes and listened attentively to the largely one-sided conversation. Of course, Helen did cut in with a few interesting comments of her own—like, "You shouldn't be driving, Pearly. The other folks on the road might not be ready to die."—that went largely unheeded.

When Pearl left, Helen said, "I'm making banana bread tomorrow. Let's remember to deliver some to Pearl tomorrow night." I was too surprised to mention that tomorrow night I would not be there, and Helen resumed the conversation we had been having before Pearl had interrupted us an hour before. She had been talking about the important things in life, which led us to discuss Mary Martha.

Helen had many friends, but Mary Martha was the one on whom she could call at any time for anything. She was the one Helen could ride the rivers with. They had been neighbors for over forty years since Helen moved to town. In earlier days, she and Mary Martha quilted together or made lye soap on the back porch. Often they sat on the front porch, talking and laughing.

Mary Martha had been taking meals to Helen ever since her surgery. Mary Martha knew Helen wouldn't want her to go to a lot of work, so she would always ask if Helen could use some leftovers or scraps. Of course, that was not what they were, but Helen liked the idea. This worked out well for both of them: Helen needed the help and Mary Martha loved to share. One meal would stretch to two or three meals. Helen loved Mary Martha's cooking; anything she fixed was good—fried potatoes, meat loaf, salmon patties, navy beans, spaghetti.

One day I went to pick up a zucchini casserole from Mary Martha's. "Helen considers you her best friend," I said after she invited me in for some coffee while we waited for the meal to finish baking.

Mary Martha smiled like a child being praised. "She's an angel," Mary Martha said. "But it's more than friendship between us. Helen treats my children as her own and has become a second grandmother to my grandchildren."

"I love how you two are always laughing," I said.

"Yes, laughter sealed our friendship," Mary Martha continued. "It's always so much fun wondering what crazy thing she'll say next."

I laughed, understanding completely.

"Or to see what crazy thing she'll do next. Like backing her car into my house."

"She did that?" I was thinking of the other evening when Helen showed me a column, "Nancy's Notes", in the local *Hale Horizons* by Nancy Schnare. She was always good for a chuckle and maybe a little inspiration. It was nothing fancy, just plain ol' country common sense from a down home lady, and Helen loved it! This time Nancy was running late to work. In her haste, she realized she hadn't even asked for God's blessings on the day, so she sat in the car and prayed, "Dear Lord, please bless this day. Please let it be a good day, and let me serve you in all I do." Then she proceeded to back the car through the closed garage door. "Lord," she prayed as she sat in her car, now embedded in plywood and siding, "this wasn't exactly what I had in mind."

"Oh, yes," Mary Martha said. "My husband, Pat, was boiling mad. He couldn't believe someone could back into a house; but I told him it could happen to anyone. The important thing was that no one got hurt."

"What did Helen say?"

Mary Martha laughed. "Typical Helen. She said, 'I'm glad your house was in the way to stop me from going into the creek.'"

I laughed all the way back to Helen's, with the hot zucchini casserole in my mittened hands.

"You have a wonderful friend," I now said to Helen about Mary Martha.

"Yes, I do," she agreed. "Mary Martha and I each know the other will stick together through bitter and sweet, through thick and thin." I smiled, but didn't mention anything about thick or thin house walls.

As Helen reminisced about some of their adventures together, a car pulled up in front of the house and Louise hurried from her car onto the side walkway. "Oh, Mother!" she said. "I'm so glad you're still up. I was hoping to catch you for at least a few minutes."

I could hardly begrudge Louise's interruption, and I stood up to welcome her. Helen herself was clearly delighted. We visited just a half hour or so, though, before Helen was ready for bed.

"Why don't I help you tonight, Mother?" Louise said, bustling in to lead Helen to the bedroom.

I sighed, and began picking up as the two walked away, chatting happily. Our last night together hadn't turned out exactly the way I had hoped, but I didn't let it bother me. I knew I'd be back to visit my new friend often.

By the time Louise came out of the bedroom, I had the kitchen cleaned up and was just heading to my reading chair.

"Esther," Louise said, sitting down across from me, "I have something to talk to you about."

I waited.

"You know how at the beginning Mother had balked at having someone come to stay with her overnight after the hip replacement surgery."

"Yes, I remember." Helen had figured her renter Lucille would be help enough. They shared the same vestibule, they were at each other's place a lot, and Lucille had been helping with meals and other small tasks—and had been willing to do more. Plus Helen had an alarm button around her neck for emergencies. She couldn't see why having someone else there was necessary.

"Well, after the first night you were here she never complained about it anymore," Louise said.

"Good." I felt pleased. "She could see that she did need help getting in and out of bed after all. She's getting along slowly now, but I think she'll be okay."

"Esther, we want you to stay on."

"You do?" I was surprised since I knew that Helen was not one to splurge, and even the small amount she was paying me must have felt like an extravagance. Perhaps I should have seen it coming, but I had been too busy preparing my mind for moving on to give much thought to staying.

"We all do. Lillie, Thelma, Harold, and I." All of Helen's children. "You can't imagine how much your presence here comforts us. We were surprised Mother took so easily to having assistance, and we think it's because she's gotten attached to you. Will you stay on?"

I didn't even need to think about it, but I did need to discuss it with Joe. Joe had always gone along with my harebrained ideas, just as I did his, and I was sure it would be the same now. Staying with Helen in the evenings didn't interfere with my daily activities. In fact, Helen often helped me prepare for my lessons—yesterday we cut out pictures for vacation Bible school projects; the week before we planned activities for the kids I teach in Sunday school. And honestly, I enjoyed staying with Helen. We read poems, discussed world problems, reviewed her photo albums and scrapbooks, made potpourri and other crafts, served tea as her neighbors and friends gathered on the porch—and did all the things that friends do together. Why would I want to give that up?

"Of course I'll stay on," I said when I called Louise the next day. "For as long as you like. Is your mother going to be okay with this arrangement?"

"I think it conveniently slipped her mind when your end date was supposed to be," Louise said with a smile. "That's what made me think to ask you this. She keeps talking as though you're never leaving."

I had to laugh. "Considering how sharp she is, I'll take that as an invitation."

It doesn't matter how old we are—there is no better feeling than acceptance.

CHAPTER 5
Looking Beyond Appearances

"When I feel like finding fault, I always begin with myself
and then I never get any farther."
DAVID GRAYSON

My staying on with Helen did not interfere with my relationship with Joe. Tuesdays, Thursdays, and Fridays I would go directly from Helen's house to class to teach in the mornings, but then Joe and I would have the rest of the day together. We would work on the farm—repairing fences, moving cattle from one pasture to another, weaning calves, mowing pasture, just checking on the cattle, and working around our house in town. When I was writing, I would run ideas past Joe, and he was always open to talking it through. On Saturdays I wouldn't go to Helen's at all, and we would have the whole evening together.

Joe was far from perfect, but he was perfect for me. He was an agriculture teacher, FFA advisor, and farmer who loved being in God's great outdoors, just as I did. We traveled some and enjoyed being together, talking and dreaming— but working hard together was our most common shared activity. Very early on I knew he was the right one for me. Ours had been a whirlwind courtship. We were in summer school at the University of Missouri, Columbia. He was working on his Master's in Agriculture and I was taking a few enrichment classes. We met at the Baptist Student Center in June, went to Denny's for lunch that day, and saw each other every day until the end of summer school. We were married September 1, 1973. I had already signed my teaching contract at Illinois Valley Community College for the 1973-74 school year, so I traveled by Amtrack every weekend to Missouri until the end of the school year.

In the first year of our marriage we bought a two hundred and forty acre farm—a hunter's paradise, with pasture for cattle, and hay fields, plus 40 acres of soybeans, with my savings and a loan from the bank. His money was being used to build a house in town. When I moved to Carrollton after our marriage, we lived in the basement of the house he was building—the inside of the upstairs was not finished for ten years. I'm sure people were wondering if it would ever be completed. That didn't bother me. It was all part of our plan.

We knew from early on that we would not be having children—all the medications Joe took affected sperm count and potency—so all our money went to the farm until it was paid off. Joe had always wanted a farm. We bought cattle, dug a well and put in a watering system for the cattle, built a large machinery shed, and bought fencing materials, a tractor and planting equipment. We later enlarged the pond that was there and constructed a larger one on the adjoining eighty acres we bought later. All extra monies went toward improving and bulldozing a small area for a home we were always going to build. That day had not yet come, but Joe had retired the same time I had—and the dream was revived.

One dreary September night as Helen sat at her sewing machine in her dining room, busily making curtains, she asked me in a playful tone, "Doesn't your husband mind that you spend five nights a week out of his bed?"

I didn't take the bait. She may be a gregarious extrovert, but that didn't mean I needed to be one. It was Helen herself who once said to me, "People are not all the same and should not try to be. If we are violets, let us be violets. If we are roses, let us be roses." It reminded me of Henry Ward Beecher's essay on God's love of different kinds of people.

No, I didn't need to take the bait. "He doesn't mind at all," I said simply. "He is very supportive of me, and glad to see me doing the things that are important to me."

She shrugged good-naturedly. "Sounds like you have a good relationship." She smiled. "Awald and I did too." She lifted her foot from the pedal and looked up. A faraway glaze came over her eyes.

Helen had frequently talked about her husband, always with great love and admiration. He had been a successful grain and livestock farmer, highly respected and loved by many. Their daughter Thelma once said to me, "Our father had the final word in the family; when he spoke, everyone listened. We had only to be told once, and it was done." Helen described him as a man with a positive outlook, always teasing and laughing.

The timing had never seemed right to ask Helen about Awald's death. I was uncomfortable approaching this topic even now, but it seemed rude not to ask about him.

"How long ago did he die?" I asked tentatively. I got up from the dining room chair where I had been sitting and was on my way to the kitchen to fix us some tea. But before I could leave, Helen continued.

"Oh, long time ago," she said, not tentative at all. "In 1960." She leaned back in her chair, curtains forgotten for now. I sat back down, teacups in hand. "It was awful. We were on our way home from the annual John Deere Day in town when we were struck by a drunken driver. Awald died after three weeks in the hospital." She had no self-pity or self-glorification in her voice, just a whole lot of feeling. I couldn't help wishing I had the guts to remember as she did. Thinking of my losses still felt like looking at the sun.

"I'm so sorry," I said. The man she had loved deeply had been ripped away from her in the ugliest of circumstances. Saying sorry seemed pitiful, but I didn't know what else to say. "Were you hurt at all?"

"Quite seriously, actually. I got a sliver of glass in my eye. It took months for the glass to work its way to the surface for the doctor to find it." Helen leaned forward and readjusted the fabric on her machine. "And yet, here I am, with eyesight better than most people's and more joy than I had believed possible."

She tapped her foot on the pedal and I might have believed she was purring. I went to get the tea.

Helen had been right after all. I did need to learn a few things from her.

My father's father, James, was a union carpenter who made sixty cents an hour or twenty-four dollars a week. When he was working, the tavern up the street got most of his paycheck. James would go to the tavern, or 'Blind Pig' as a saloon was called, after work on Friday and came home Sunday evening to beat the kids and their mother. Monday morning he returned to his job. But when he was laid off, which was often, they had even less to eat.

I don't know what it was that triggered the telling of this story to Helen, but she immediately identified with it.

"My grandfather Henry had the same problem," Helen said as she leaned back with the tea I had just brought her. "Nobody talked about it though. His case was an example of how a very nice person can become so consumed with a desire to drink that he becomes a menace to all his loved ones. If it had only been his wife's life that was affected, she probably could have put up with it, but it was too much for the kids. She told him to leave. What else could she do?"

"Yes, it's the kids who suffer," I replied. And the grandkids whose father is too beaten down to be able to give love to his own kids. But I didn't say that out loud. Besides, things had really improved by the time I came along. "My father's maternal grandfather, Grandpa Baker, after William and Arthur were there about a month, said to Grandma Baker, "Don't take them. They will turn out to be drunkards like their dad." The children returned to Springfield on a train. But not one of them ever drank a drop of alcohol. The two younger children were two and four and probably didn't remember as much."

I sat for a while thinking about my father. He admired Abraham Lincoln. I guess he thought they had a lot in common, growing up poor and overcoming much. When Lincoln was born in 1809, a neighbor held him and said he didn't think the little guy would ever come to much. We can all testify to the contrary.

"Everyone deserves a second chance," Helen said. She set her cup down and started back to work on the sewing machine.

This prompted me to tell Helen about my great aunt who, in the early 1900s, as a 26 year old, became pregnant by a traveling evangelist of the local holiness church founded by her father. Of course, this revelation became hush, hush. So my great aunt went away to work in an orphanage in Carlinville until the baby boy was born at a hospital in Quincy. The wonderful thing was that the baby was adopted into the family of a brother and his wife who had no children of their own. I could imagine my great aunt watching him grow up and eventually having children and grandchildren of his own.

Nevertheless, my aunt was shunned by her deeply Christian relatives. She never married, spent her whole life helping on the farm and in later years cared for her aging parents. She was known for raising horehound, a medicinal herb with little white flowers, celery which she covered to keep from the sun, and dahlias.

"It is sad," Helen said, "because people could not forgive and treat her as Jesus did those when he walked this earth. "He who is without sin, cast the first stone." They couldn't understand the whole situation. So we have to forgive them of their ignorance."

Helen could remember unfortunate situations from her own past. "We tend to look down on others because they seem to not possess the virtues we think they should have, but they may be pleasing to God for others reasons which we do not know," she said.

Every year since 1985 during the second week of September, Helen made cider. And not just Helen. It was a big event at Lillie and Gene's farm near DeWitt, ten miles east of Carrollton. All the family on both sides—the Audsleys and the Raasches—came, plus much of Lillie's neighborhood. This involved fifty or more people. Lillie's daughter Jeannie would often bring foreign exchange students for the get-together— from Japan, Chile, Germany, Finland, Sweden, Norway, Denmark, and England.

Lillie and Gene had a nice orchard of twelve or so trees, which usually supplied the apples they needed; if not, they bought extra. "It is important to have the right blend," Lillie once explained to me, "—usually Jonathan, which are a little tart and Golden Delicious. We also add Jonagold or Gala." All fall apples. The Red Delicious left a red color to the batch. It didn't affect the flavor, just changed the color. The apples were crisp, not soft or mealy— picked the week before.

They set up a wash and cull system. The apples were put in large galvanized washtubs and then separated into cider and non-cider piles.

"That's my job," Helen told me as we sat in her kitchen with Lillie, who had come to talk through the upcoming day's events with her mother.

"Yes, Mother ramrodded the culling," Lillie said laughing.

"Someone has to be in charge," Helen said as she smoothed the fall colored table cloth. "You young people use perfectly good apples for cider when they could be used for other things." She turned to me. "I take home a bunch of those apples, and cook them up for Mary Martha, Pearl, and Wilma."

"She's not as bad as she sounds," Lillie said to me as she got up to refill her mother's coffee. "Actually, everyone wants to be where Mother is. She and Aunt Lucille laugh up a storm."

"How is it that you get along with everyone, Helen?" I asked. I walked to the window and adjusted the shade to let more sun in the house.

"Simple," Helen said. "I just don't attend every argument I'm invited to."

We all laughed, and then I turned to Lillie. "So what happens after you pry the apples loose from your mother's grasp."

"See," Helen said, "I'm declining that invitation."

"After the culling comes the cutting," Lillie said, laughing. Eight to ten people take them out of the water, cull more, and cut out the bad spots. The cut apples are then put into ten to twelve wire baskets and stored in a dozen and a half cardboard boxes or four gallon milk crates.

Six men take the cut apples and use an old time cider press to grind them.

The apples fall through the machine to be mashed—and then fall into a basket. The press screws down and the juice flows into a plastic tub. Gene uses a 2 x 4 cheater to squeeze the knobs tighter to get more juice. The pulp is dumped out onto the field and the juice is strained—twice, using cheese cloth or an old sheer curtain—into five gallon buckets.

This juice is then poured into a blending container so the various apple flavors will blend well. Then cider is put into clean water jugs, a special label with the date affixed, and it is ready. They make over a hundred gallons of cider at a time, so everyone takes home as much as they can use.

The fun isn't over yet, though. "After all the work is done, we have a giant wiener roast," Lillie said.

"And we roast marshmallows," Helen added.

"We even set up a screened in 'cook tent' to prepare all the side dishes."

Travelers set up tents out in the yard or bring campers. Others sleep on the floor in the house. The three bedrooms and living room are all filled with mats and sleeping bags. One little tyke always liked it under the kitchen table; perhaps he felt safer there. Lillie said that twice she and her husband Gene went to town and stayed in a motel because the others liked staying up playing cards, laughing and talking into the wee hours of the morning. Neighbors went home for sleeping, but were back for breakfast—which was the highlight of the event for many: biscuits and gravy, fried mush, bacon and eggs, toast and jelly. They were usually heading home by noon that second day.

"A couple times we had rainstorms," Lillie said, "but that didn't stop us. We set up shop in the barn and had an attached canopy tent put up."

"We never missed a year," Helen said.

I had been standing by the window all this time—it felt better to be on my feet—and I saw an ambulance racing down Benton Street. Little kids looked up from their chalk drawings on the sidewalk and cars pulled to the side of the road.

"Sounds like you all choose to interrupt life rather than let life interrupt you." I said. "How wonderful!" My family never gathered together to make cider. However, we did gather at my grandma and grandpa's for hog butchering days, an annual Halloween party in the garage, sleighing, horseback riding, playing in the creek, parties for making miniature dolls from red and pink hollyhock petals, get-togethers every few weeks when we played a million different games. The memories kept flooding back.

"Hog butchering days were a real learning experience for us cousins," I told

Helen. "But it was mainly the fun of being together, the talking and laughing, the camaraderie, the sense of being family."

Helen was quick to interject her memories on the subject. "I remember how the preparation began several days ahead. We built a small trench filled with dry firewood ready to be lit. Later huge black kettles were placed on a stand over the trench. The men mounted a very stout pole trestle to handle the 250 pound hog carcasses. The smokehouse was readied for the hams and bacon to be hung for smoking."

"Do you recall how much everyone looked forward to butchering days?" I laughingly interjected as we both relived our excitement. "We were up before 4 a.m. so we would not miss anything."

At this Helen came to life. Excitement was running through her veins. "I think we used every part of the pig except the squeal. I suppose, if we had been a bit more imaginative we could have found some use for it as well. Very little was wasted back then when money was very scarce and people actually knew what hunger was. The head was cooked, ground and cooked again with cornmeal to make scrapple to fry. With maple syrup on top, it became a mainstay of winter breakfasts on the farm."

"The meat that could not be cured or eaten right away was canned in glass jars after packing in hot lard. Meat undesirable for use as ham, bacon or pork chops was converted into sausage and stuffed into casings from the intestines." Lillie, her daughter, later told me that Helen would be in the center of each job. She wanted to make sure everything was done properly. And she could keep up with the hardest workers on the crew.

"Generally the hogs were completely butchered and hanging on the pole frames by noon so we could be ready for a hearty dinner of fresh liver, which we kids fought over, and tenderloin, mashed potatoes, gravy, biscuits, green beans and homemade pies," Helen added.

Excess fat from the pigs was cut into cubes and cooked down for use as lard in frying and baking. Anything left after the fat was cooked out became cracklings, crunchy little morsels the children devoured like potato chips.

In the final stage Helen and her crew added lye to the remaining lard to make soap. The light brown soap could clean almost everything. "We grated it with a metal cabbage cutter to make small pieces that would dissolve in a washing machine."

"The greatest thing," Helen said as she finished her recollection, "was the festive atmosphere. It seems that the big family and neighborhood get-togethers have gone by the wayside, just like frugality and simplicity."

I remained standing by the window as Helen and Lillie moved into the other room, chatting happily. A memory had flooded my mind an instant after I shook off my twinge of jealousy.

I was ten or eleven. It was twenty years after the Great Depression. My grandparents wanted to celebrate the memory of the good times as well as the bad times. It was like the Jewish feast of the Booths in the Bible. The Israelites celebrated by living in little shacks to remember what their ancestors had gone through during their forty years of wandering in the wilderness before they reached the Promised Land.

Everyone came. There were probably forty aunts, uncles, and cousins there. I remember eating raccoon and cornbread and beans, drinking water from canning jars, using odds and ends for utensils, and filling lamps with kerosene for light. The laughter was what made the evening great.

Grandma had wanted us to remember, and I had nearly forgotten.

Nearly.

CHAPTER 6
Finding Freedom in Simplicity

"The wise man carries his possessions within him."
BIAS OF PRIENE (6TH CENT. B.C.)

"Your petunias are still blooming," I said as I watered Helen's flowers a few days after she returned from cider making. It was already the end of September. "How do you keep them so healthy?"

"You need to fertilize and remove the dead blooms regularly," she called from the porch. Helen had been an avid gardener in her day. Her mother, Katie, and her grandmother, Mary, also had large gardens with fruit trees. Now Helen's daughter Lillie had a large garden and fruit trees. "I'm not able to care for them like I used to, and there aren't as many blooms now."

"Looks good to me," a youthful looking woman, probably in her sixties, called out. Helen laughed and waved as the woman walked down the driveway toward the house. "I saw you here on the porch and thought I'd stop by," she said.

Helen introduced me to Eleanor saying that their friendship went back to childhood days. "While growing up, I always looked forward to someone saying, 'Let's go to the Raasches,'" Eleanor said. "We felt welcome and had so much fun at Helen's house. Not much has changed."

Eleanor visited for just a few minutes and then went on her way.

Helen picked up two letters sent by dear friends from the little white table by her chair on the porch and settled in to read them. I smiled at her as I removed a couple of dead leaves from the pink geraniums near me.

"It's good to have a friend," she called out to me, "but having several friends is like whipped cream on the strawberry shortcake."

The next morning, as I was preparing to leave, Helen was still in bed at 7 a.m. when the phone rang. Her bedroom is next to the living room, where I slept, with no door. This helped me keep an eye on her even when I was in bed.

"That must be Wilma with the latest scoop," Helen said. "She's the only one who calls this early." Wilma was another who had been Helen's friend for more than forty years. They were neighbors from the country. Wilma now lived in a quaint little house on Main Street, a fitting place amidst a lot of activity—just what Wilma loved. She usually knew about everything going on in our small town. She had many friends and talked on the phone a lot—and she loved to be the first to know and the first to tell.

Helen's phone was on her headboard so it was easy to reach. She had a phone in each room of the house and a portable one she kept in her bag on the walker—as talking on the phone was a primary way she kept up her support system.

"Well, good morning, Wilma," I heard Helen say. I was ready to leave, but I waited a few more moments to say goodbye. While they chatted—with Helen mostly providing verbal nods of her head—I was reminded of a bit of news that I could give Helen before anyone could have told Wilma.

"I have something you can be first to tell Wilma for a change," I said as soon as Helen hung up. "The two houses across the street from her house are going to be torn down." My church had recently purchased the property with the idea of making room for a parking lot or an educational building.

Helen didn't take the bait. "It would be better to let Wilma think she knew it first," is all she said.

I was glad she was in bed and couldn't see me blush. I should have known better.

When I left a few minutes later, I bumped into Florence, a neatly dressed, pretty woman in her fifties and one of Helen's many neighbors. She was in a hurry, as always. It's a wonder she found time to chat with anyone. "How's our little friend today?" she asked.

"Just as saintly as ever," I said honestly. Not that Helen was perfect. Just like the rest of us, she had shortcomings. She had little toleration for the lazy who could work but who lived off the taxpayer. She was impatient with people who did not live up to their commitments, who turned their backs when the road got rutted. She often had less than kind comments about spendthrifts—those who wasted things or threw out items that could be repaired or cleaned. I'm sure it all went back to that work ethic that had been drilled into her in her childhood. Her daughter Louise said she was stubborn and bullheaded. She certainly did tell it like it was, or at least like she saw it.

Still, Florence laughed warmly, and I knew she understood the delights and frustrations of her practically perfect neighbor. Florence was a ready-made basket of information about Helen. "I'm going to tell you something," Florence said. "I never told Helen because I didn't want to spoil her fun."

"What's that?"

"A while back, I saw Ms. Helen come out of her house carrying a large shopping bag. She shuffled over to Tom's house over there—" Tom lived to the east of Helen "—and walked up onto the porch. There she left the bag and hurried home."

"What do you suppose was in it?"

"I don't just suppose," Florence said, her voice lowering intimately. "My curiosity got the better of me, and I walked up on the neighbor's porch to see what was in the bag. To my surprise, it was full of red ripe apples. Pinned to the bag was an unsigned note reading, 'Enjoy.'"

I laughed. "Typical Helen," I said. "Those must be the apples that she culled from those being thrown into the vat to make cider."

Florence nodded. "We all need a saint like her around so we can believe there's hope in this old world, don't we?"

"That's absolutely true, Florence," I said. It absolutely was.

"Oh, don't throw that away," Helen said, as I was tossing out a piece of used aluminum foil. "That's the good, heavy foil. I can use that later." Helen spent her life doing what people of her generation learned early—making do, creating something out of nothing, never wasting anything. She gardened on a shoestring—saving seeds from the year before and sharing bulbs and seeds with neighbors. She even made potpourri by simmering orange, lemon, and grapefruit peels with spices. It was a delightful citrus smell, redolent of just-peeled oranges.

That little aluminum foil incident prompted me to tell Helen about my Uncle William who, during the gas rationing days of WWII, hung a little placard on the rear view mirror in his old Chevy truck stating, "Is this trip really necessary?"

"Sounds like a good idea even for today," she chuckled.

While Helen was growing up, her family saved for what they wanted. They waited, saving for months before making any major purchases. The only time she and her husband, Awald, owed money was when they bought the farms. Even those debts were soon paid off, a remarkable feat while raising four children. When they were short on cash, they'd sell some calves.

"Few things are needed to make one content. So-called bargains may simply be traps to fall into," Helen would say. She never owned a credit card. "Some think I'm crazy, but I'm not. I can live without them." She lived comfortably and did not yearn for more—unlike her former neighbor who had a building built just for her huge collections that must have taken a lifetime to collect. Still, Helen had wanted me to go to that neighbor's estate auction "just to see."

"I met three marble collectors who had come all the way from Kokomo, Indiana," I'd reported.

"They must have all lost their marbles," she said with that famous grin of hers.

I'd laughed, and then asked seriously. "Why do you think people like to collect things?"

"It's just human nature."

"Have you ever seen a hearse hauling a U-Haul behind it?" I'd asked.

She'd laughed and said, "That's one way to look at it." This philosophy reminded me of a passage from Henry Wadsworth Longfellow: "In character, in manners, in style, in all things, the supreme excellence is simplicity."

Helen was now on the phone with Pearl saying I would be right over with some applesauce. The banana bread hadn't turned out just right and Helen insisted we'd just have to eat that on our own. It tasted fine to me, and I happily anticipated not letting it go to waste.

What I wasn't anticipating so eagerly was spending time with Pearl. But when she opened her door widely she welcomed me in—"Any friend of Helen's is a friend of mine"—I accepted her offer to join her for tea.

We sat down together in her spacious, simple kitchen at a table across from each other, I with my own uncertain expectations of how the conversation would go, and she probably had reservations, too.

Before long, Pearl was telling me her life story. She came from a family of thirteen children. Her father had been a drunk who had often been gone for days at a time. Her mother had the responsibility of providing and caring for the children by herself. Neighbors did help, but life was tough for Pearl. They lived in a chicken house with a dirt floor. Two of her brothers died during the 1918 influenza epidemic and were buried in the same coffin. Helen remembered several neighbors who went to sit with the family. "Family and friends sitting up with the sick or dead was common practice in those days. They would stay all night ready to comfort if needed."

Of course, Pearl's neighbors were also devastated by this deadly outbreak. I later learned it killed an estimated 650,000 in the U.S. alone and 20 million worldwide with one billion ill—one-fifth of the world's population. Of the 4.3 million Americans who served in WWI, 126,000 died. Only 50,000 died in battle; the rest died from disease, especially influenza. The epidemic traveled west from Europe, beginning in the Eastern U.S., and spread to forty-six states. People were struck with the illness and some just died on the street. It was simply a struggle for air until they suffocated.

Pearl had lived through this time period and was clearly still bearing the effects of this traumatic time. She talked about it at great lengths, surprisingly comfortable with sharing intimate details with me, a virtual stranger.

I felt sorry for Pearl, but I still didn't like her much. I couldn't help comparing my first encounter with Helen to this one. Helen had talked nothing of herself and Pearl had talked entirely of herself.

When I got up to leave, Pearl said, "Do you like tomatoes?" She picked a few from her garden and handed them to me. "Take these and give some to Helen." I smiled. Deep down, Pearl was a good person, but it was hard for her to show it.

Perhaps Helen sent me over there not only to deliver applesauce.

Helen and I shared many stories as we piddled around in the kitchen. Tonight she was cleaning the top burners of the stove. When she was done, they sparkled. I wanted to help, but she wanted to keep at her small chores as long as she could.

Helen told me about Rachel, her former neighbor from the country. Rachel heard about the plight of so many abused and traumatized children and wondered what she could do to help. She came up with the idea of buying dolls and stuffed animals at garage sales, repairing them, cleaning them, and giving them anonymously to hospitals and other places so these gifts could be distributed to little ones who needed to be comforted. "Now people bring dolls to Rachel to lovingly repair," Helen said.

I was impressed. "Didn't King Solomon say, 'The one who blesses others is abundantly blessed; the one who helps others is helped?'"

Helen spouted eloquently on the subject, having seen this concept proved true in her own life. "If we can help people find a way of giving suited to them, we have done a wonderful service."

Even in this she wasn't thinking of the endless times she herself gave to others.

I remember the time Helen gave by way of small talk: Carrie, a mere acquaintance, talked for fifteen minutes about an elm tree that she had someone remove. "They had to bring special equipment. They tore up the yard getting there. It had been dying, with fewer leaves coming out each passing year." And on and on she went. When she finished the story, we knew everything there was to know about that tree. Were we any better off for that conversation? I doubt it. But Helen had the patience to listen and gave another person great honor in the process.

Again, the extraordinary came shining through the ordinary. It reminded me of Jesus turning the water into wine.

No wonder so many have honored Helen as much as they did. She talked when she had something important to say and she listened when someone else did—and she took action when the talk had gone on too long.

But this, too, is not the main reason I'm crying at her funeral.

CHAPTER 7
It's in the Little Things

"The common tasks are beautiful if we have eyes
to see their shining ministry."
GRACE NOLL CROWELL

My favorite photograph of Helen is one of her at age eighty, riding in a speedboat with her grandson and great-grandson, with the wind blowing through her silver hair. And to think I had once been worried that this house would be a place of demise.

"You must love boating!" I said to her the first time I noticed the picture.

"Nah," she said. "It's just that they invited me. I didn't want to let the world pass me by."

Helen's love of life was contagious. I found myself wanting to be more adventuresome—which was not typical of me. I had been holding back for so much of my life up to this point, never wanting to fully engage for fear of being hurt. And I had good reason.

Take Joe's health for instance. We always joked about how I would someday marry a younger man after he died off, but in truth I was terrified that he really would disappear from my life. My husband had health problems early on from the time I first met him. He took several medications for high blood pressure, some for gout, acid reflux disease, rheumatoid arthritis, and sky-high triglycerides, others for the heart—morning and evening. He had severe headaches and sinus problems and took medicine for those too. One of the side effects from the necessary medicine was severe muscle aches and pain. The back corner of our kitchen counter became his medicine shop. Besides that, his father had died of a heart attack at the age of fifty-seven. I loved Joe more than any other person on earth, but I knew to hold him loosely.

Actually, all of God's gifts are ours for only a short time and we are prudent to hold onto them loosely. Timothy tells us that things of this world are so uncertain, and we should lay up treasures in heaven so that we may take hold of the life that is truly life.

And yet by embracing that philosophy, I had somehow missed out on embracing life. I still wasn't sure how to find the balance.

It's not that I never stuck my neck out. We did try to have children even though we knew the chances were slim. That was probably the most risky thing I've ever done. I should clarify here. Previously I had said we knew from early on that we would not be having children. That is not quite accurate. We knew from early on that it would be difficult to have children, but we both loved children so much and did not easily give up the dream. My husband especially loved children. He would go up to any baby or little child, no matter where, and they would always let him pick them up. It was quite beautiful. Everyone was amazed by his way with kids. He was the only man at our church who worked in the nursery Sunday mornings.

And so we kept hoping. There was a chance, after all. "It's not that the possibility is non-existent," Joe would say to me. I kept track of my monthly ovulation schedule faithfully and we were intimate at the scheduled times.

Nothing.

We never considered fertility clinics. We felt that God knew what was going on and what was best. Fertility clinics were good for some; they just weren't for us. Maybe the real reason was we were just too busy to take the time.

But again we stuck our necks out by attempting to adopt a child. We went through the whole process to take in a foster child—taking interviews and classes—with the hope later of adopting this child. At the last moment, however, an aunt and uncle decided to raise the girl. This was a big disappointment for both of us, and we did not proceed with any further application.

Losing the opportunity to welcome that girl into our home was nothing short of gut-wrenching. A feeling of inadequacy overwhelmed me, and I'm not sure I've ever lost that feeling.

The last thing I could have done was set myself up for that kind of disappointment again.

All that to say, I did have good reason to not get in that figurative motor boat—but the more time I spent with Helen, the more I actually wanted to.

The second and third weekends in November during deer season were permanently reserved for Joe to go hunting with his college buddy Gene and Gene's son Gary. They had come from St. Louis every year for thirty-five years without miss during those two weekends. Sometimes Gene's wife, Jane, also came. Gene and Joe used to go coon hunting near Columbia when they were students and during Joe's early teaching years. We would visit Gene and Jane periodically and their family would come visit us, but the highlight of their interaction was this hunting trip. These guys would get geared up for it all year long. As the time approached, they oiled their guns, purchased the right ammunition, read hunting magazines, and talked for hours on the phone about the sighting of deer and tracks on the farm. They planned their strategy.

I had learned to like hunting by now, but mostly because I enjoyed spending time in the outdoors with Joe. Sometimes during deer season Joe and I would be in a deer stand or sitting near a tree, but those two weekends were for Joe and his buddies alone.

I shot a deer once. That was never the thrill for me. The thrill was watching the deer, or turkeys, or rabbits on our hunter's paradise. One time we saw over 120 turkeys in a group. We tried to count them. Another time five deer stopped about six feet in front of us as we were sitting at the foot of a big burr oak on the north edge of our property line. Wow! Now that was exciting. They looked around, but I don't think they saw us because they simply pranced off gingerly after a few minutes.

I was glad to see Gene again this year because Joe so enjoyed this camaraderie with his longtime friend. He'd been having a tough time with his health, and I knew this weekend would provide a little pick-me-up for him. Besides, I didn't mind having a little quiet time to myself.

After sending them off with full stomachs and a crock-pot full of hot beef stew, which they plugged in at the machinery shed, I planned the evening meal for the hungry hunters when they returned. After making the dessert and salad, and seeing that I had everything I needed for the rest of the meal, I spent time reading, one of my favorite activities. It was a nice, quiet time—a lull before the storm—when the wild tales of deer sightings and tracking deer for miles began. The storm usually included showing off the racks collected that day and making big plans for the next day.

And I was right: Joe slept with a smile that night.

It was the second week of December, and I was glad to enter Helen's warm house. The smell of fresh baked bread hung in the air like a homey wake-up call. I could almost taste the toasty coffee we were soon going to share. The weather was mild for mid-Missouri—we were still awaiting our first real snowfall—but I had a chill. It was more than that though, my rushing into Helen's haven. I wanted to be there. I looked forward to the surprises I found in her stories that left me reflecting on my life, and life in general. Each day was a new adventure in how surprising the ordinary could be.

"Anybody home?" I hollered as I came in the front door so Helen would know I had arrived and not be startled. In the winter Helen was usually in the kitchen picking out pecans, reading the newspaper, or doing the supper dishes. Today she was reading.

"Nobody home," she answered, glancing up with a warm smile. "They just left."

"Where'd they go?" I asked as I pulled off my coat and hung it on the coat rack. I threw my little overnight bag on the floor next to the bed and walked quickly to the kitchen.

"Off to Timbuktu," she replied. This exchange had become a ritual. Helen had a million different answers.

I plopped down in a chair across from where Helen was reading. When she looked up, I smiled. "Helen, how would you like to write a Christmas letter to send to all your friends and relatives? I could help you." Christmas decorations were in full display around town. The church choir was in the midst of preparation for the Christmas cantata. The paper had already announced Santa's upcoming visits around the square. I was ready for festivities myself.

"Are you kidding?" Helen went back to her newspaper.

"I know writing's not your favorite activity," I said, "but I'll help." Helen did not go to high school like her younger brother and sisters. "I was needed at home," she once told me, "and it just didn't work out." But she continued reading and got her real education in the trenches—day by day, little by little.

"Uh uh," Helen said, shaking her head. "Everyone would see right through it and know it was someone else's doings, not mine."

"They may realize you had help, but they would know you were sincere in your greetings."

"They would all think I'd become senile in my old age."

"I see. Pretending to be someone other than who you are is not your cup of tea." I stood up and went to the kitchen to pour myself some coffee. "I think this is something you would enjoy, but I admire you for daring to be just who you are without doctoring up the impression."

Helen chuckled. She folded the pages of her newspaper neatly on her lap. "That's just the way I am, plain and simple. That way I have no fear of being found out. That's the same way you are, my dear."

I grunted, still a little sore she hadn't accepted my idea. I poured more coffee in my favorite of Helen's mugs, the one with the Heidelberg Castle. It reminded me of our common German heritage and the time I lived with the Klein family in Koblenz. I then brought the carafe over to refill her cup.

As soon as I sat down in my usual place across from Helen in her homey, old-fashioned living room, liberally spread with lace doilies, Helen continued. "From the first day I met you, I knew you had no pretensions." She smiled a little mischievously. "Secrets, yes. Pretensions, no."

Startled, I pulled back. "Secrets?" I didn't have any secrets. My life was an open book.

Helen simply nodded, still smiling a little.

"My only secret is that I'm not as sweet as I look," I said, trying to make the moment light.

She waited, steepling her fingers.

I got more serious. "Actually, that's really true. I'm so task-oriented that I tend to neglect the little things in relationships. But you're helping me with that."

She closed her eyes for just a moment and shook her head ever so slightly, as if I were a student who answered incorrectly. Then she flashed a smile and moved on. I had often done the same thing when a student simply couldn't understand the words I had been saying in the language he or she was trying to learn. In this case, however, I didn't know what I had missed.

"You're right," Helen said. "The little things are important: a card, a letter, a phone call, or just sitting and listening. I think you're the one teaching me that." She set the folded newspaper on the little table beside her. "Maybe we *should* do Christmas cards. But let's make individual cards for all those on my list; that would be more my style than the letter."

"Sounds like fun." I was glad for the focus to have switched away from me. "Let's write up a list now. I'll bring my craft supplies tomorrow and we'll get started on your design for the cards then."

"Maybe I could even add a little gift."

I nodded, catching the vision. "You could sew a little appliquéd tree ornament, like the appliqués you used to make on quilts with Mary Martha."

A half hour later I was trying not to listen to the hypnotic tick-tock of the pendulum clocks when Clara and Sally popped in with Christmas cookies, laughing and giggling like teenagers. These ladies were two of Helen's friends from her old Amigo Club—a neighborhood club begun around 1940 where women could be together and share good times.

Helen was always ready for stories and gladly welcomed them in. They talked and munched cookies, talked some more, laughed, and told more stories. They probed me with questions, of course, apparently a little puzzled at my role at Helen's. Helen set them straight real quick. "You're just jealous because you don't have a teacher on your premises."

They moved on quickly. Clara told about their club's Christmas gift exchange one year. "Helen gave me a large red compote dish. She tried to rub out the price, but the paint came off in a small area. When I unwrapped it, she apologized, but said she was going to give it to me anyway."

"Yes, well—" Helen began.

"And I'm so glad she did," Clara continued, laughing. "It is beautiful. I smile every time I put fruit into it—and think of my sweet Helen."

They talked about being good neighbors in the country. Sally said, "If you are a good neighbor, you will also have good ones wherever you are. Your neighbors are about as good as you expect them to be."

I imagine that more good is achieved at such neighborhood get-togethers like the Amigo Club than is accomplished all day in a doctor's office.

CHAPTER 8
Happiness is a By-Product of Love

"When you sow love, joy grows. "
GERMAN PROVERB

The next evening when I opened Helen's heavy oak glass-encased front door, I detected a delicious, cinnamon-like smell permeating the house—a fresh-baked-cookies aroma with undertones of roasted peanuts. No wonder I loved walking into Helen's house so much.

"Anybody home?"

"I'd say about three thousand people in Carrollton are," Helen called. "Or at least they should be on a night like this."

I walked into the kitchen where Louise was helping Helen with Christmas gifts for the grandkids. We greeted each other warmly and chatted a bit about school—where I had spent so much of my life and where Louise still worked—meanwhile munching on Helen's fresh-from-the-oven snickerdoodles.

When Louise headed home, Helen said, "You talk about your classroom a lot. Do you ever wish you hadn't retired yet?"

I probably talked about my teaching more than I thought I did. Work had been my life. "No," I said. "It was time for me to go." If I hadn't retired, I never would have had the experiences with Helen that were enriching my life so much.

The other evening Helen's son, Harold, and I had been talking about his retirement, and I turned the question on Helen. "When do you plan to retire,

Helen?" I'd teased.

Harold slapped his knee. "Mother retire?" he said. "That'll never happen."

"Not likely," she agreed, "but sometimes I do get tired. Does that mean if I get tired again, I'm retired?"

"It's a groaner, Mother," Harold said. But he laughed. Corny or not, Helen could always get people to laugh.

We were not short on laughter this evening either as we got ready to make Christmas cards. "Okay, girls, let's get this show on the road," Helen said.

Lucille and Helen had worked on the appliqués that day, and we got busy designing, cutting, and pasting. Each card was uniquely designed with the recipient in mind.

"I never get tired of Christmas," Helen said as she picked up the scissors.

Even without the snow, the season was certainly upon us. Helen's grandkids were making plans for coming home. Her son, Harold, was chopping wood at Lillie's for his fireplace. Her best friend Mary Martha had just called to ask about coming with them to the Christmas program at church. The abundance of Helen's life was never more evident.

Her excitement reminded me of my own childhood. My grandmother did many things that made us grandkids feel special. At our Christmas gatherings, she would take us "fishing for gifts," as she called it. She used to hang up a sheet and sit behind it, putting little gifts on the line for the grandkids as we awaited our turn to go fishing. We held our fishing pole so the line would be on the other side of the sheet. She then tied a little gift to the end of our line. When she was ready, she gave it a little tug. That was our cue to pull up the gift. It was a fun time.

"I can still hear my grandmother's cheery, 'Ho! Ho! Ho! Merry Christmas!' as she came into the house dressed as Santa Claus for our Christmas get-togethers," I said as I drew more outlines for Helen to cut.

"You must be talking about your Grandma Mathilda," Helen said, looking up from her cutting. I was impressed by her memory—and listening skills.

"Yes, she made every occasion special. I remember gathering around her as she listened to us recite our lines for the Christmas program at church and sipping hot chocolate later. I don't remember much of what we talked about, but I remember it produced wholesome laughter and a sense of security and togetherness."

"It's funny how the senses evoke memories," Helen said. She didn't stop working as she talked. "I can still smell the fragrance of the lilac bushes in our back yard when I was a child and the delicious aroma of the cinnamon rolls my grandmother Mary made every morning."

"Yeah, I know what you mean," I said enjoying the feel of the velvet appliqué under my fingers. "Just the other day I heard some kids laughing in the distance, and I was transported back to those days when I was one of the laughing kids."

"Doing what?"

I laughed. "We were on our way to Grandma and Grandpa's on Christmas Day 1948 in a sled my dad made from slab lumber with the bark on one side that he got from the nearby sawmill. My dad was good at coming up with something in a pinch, and he didn't want us to miss out on our long awaited get-together with all the cousins. He nailed the slabs together to form a 10' by 16' sled."

"How did he pull it?"

"He tied the sled to the 1945 John Deere B tractor with log chains. With straw bales piled to keep out the snow and plenty of blankets, we were off. A little thing like two feet of snow wasn't going to keep us from our rendezvous," I said as I picked out more sequins to finish the card for Florence.

"That's a good one," Helen said. She reached for the glue and yarn. "We haven't touched on taste yet—and that's a powerful sense. I can still taste the cold water from the hand pump as I drank from the tin cup, or the snow ice cream we made," Helen said, beaming.

I could almost taste it myself.

"I remember catching my first fish," Helen continued, "and almost falling into the water when my little sister Lucille fell asleep on the dead tree lying across the pond. I pulled her up by her bonnet before her head went under. I remember not wanting to go fishing for awhile after that."

I told Helen how my dad and his brother remembered frying bacon on an upside down tub in the grassy field by their house when they were four and six. "They would start a grass fire, turn the tub over, and fry bacon on it. The kids all said it was the best bacon they had ever eaten. It's amazing how one remembers things. Don't you think our taste memories are tainted with the excitement of the moment?" I asked.

Helen nodded and picked up another card and appliqué. "Yes, I know that's true—and just being kids, you feel more. I still believe that nobody ever made peach and apricot pies like my mother did."

"I vividly remember the peck or so of loose bananas 'on their last leg' that Dad brought home on occasion from the market in St. Louis where he sold the cantaloupes we raised. They were a treat, and we gobbled them up." I held up the card I had finished and admired it.

"You remember those bananas tasting so good because of the excitement and memories of seeing the pleasure on your dad's face when he entered the house with that big box," Helen said.

I continued to cut the paper for Helen's cards. By now quite a little stack was forming, but we carried on. "My brother, Glen, thinks it's because the bananas really were better then. New varieties have since been developed to withstand the shipment. Like those tomatoes which are picked green and shipped to the Midwest from California, they just don't taste as good as the home-grown ones."

"I remember the yummy ice cream we bought at Leta's Store," Helen said. Leta was the wife of the man who built the post office in 1876. When the post office moved to town, the building was turned into a general store and later was moved to what is now the junction of Highway 139 and Route 24. "John Tatham and his wife lived upstairs and ran the store," Helen said. "You could get Rainbow bread, ice, and other staples. The Coca-Cola box was always full of a large assortment of soda pop. It was sort of the neighborhood gathering place—fireworks on the Fourth of July, picnics, traveling shows. The kids would buddy up to Mr. Tatham because they knew he would give them a cookie or a piece of candy. The hunters tried to make it back to Leta's Store at noon because they looked forward to a half inch slice of bologna and cheese on two slices of bread and a Pepsi, all for twenty-five cents."

"Strange how memories work," I said. "Last night I was doing a crossword puzzle, and the answer to one of the items was 'Kochkäse.' That's a German word for a cooked cottage cheese I heard my mother use when I was young. I had not heard it for over forty years, but all of a sudden it came to my mind."

"Perhaps all the things we ever did or the thoughts we ever had are in our memory, and we just need the right spark to bring them forth," Helen said as she continued to fold the cards. The cards were beginning to pile up. I would bring envelopes tomorrow.

"Oh, look!" I said, interrupting our conversation. The little sheep and donkey designs I had discovered were clever. "Don't you think Louise will love this?" Helen agreed, and I quickly engrossed myself in making new designs. My artistic bent was returning. I was enjoying this activity even more than I thought I would.

"What are you and Joe doing for Christmas?" Helen asked.

The question startled me—but I quickly composed myself. "Oh, we'll go back to Illinois to gather with all of Grandma Mathilda's children, grandchildren, great-grandchildren, and great-great-grandchildren at Granny's Café in Chapin—but not until after Christmas—to allow everyone the opportunity to spend Christmas Day with their immediate families." I knew I had evaded her question, and so I tried again. "Before that Joe and I will go to the Christmas Eve service and the Christmas morning service. We were always welcome at my sister's or brother's or at various church families for their family get-togethers, but we preferred a quiet evening meal together at home as usual."

"Just the two of you?" she asked a bit too casually. It was the closest she had come to prying, but I was a master at deflecting even direct questions of this sort. I didn't owe it to anyone to have to explain my situation—and the sort of memories she was attempting to pull from me now were not fun to recall.

"Oh, I doubt we'll have much time alone—you know how Christmas is." We had been very busy with other activities—parties, concerts, parades, etc. during the season. Besides, we were leaving soon for the big, after-Christmas celebration. I kept busy and hardly noticed the absence in my life. But there was always that little twinge of regret.

It's a line I said to most people so they wouldn't get that concerned expression on their faces as they thought of my Christmas without kids. And what I said was mostly true. But when Helen didn't respond, I suddenly felt guilty. She knew I was evading the question.

Besides, I hardly even accepted it myself that my lack of love for the holidays was anything more than frustration with the rampant commercialization of it, the ridiculous straying from the true meaning of Christmas.

But maybe it was more than that.

"I'm tired," Helen said after a few moments. "I think I'll take a little break." She pushed the craft items to the side, leaned back, and closed her eyes.

I took the laundry out of the dryer and brought it to Helen to help fold. She generally liked helping. The usual active conversation, however, was noticeably absent as we worked.

"Oh, Esther," she said absently just before folding the last towel. "Would you be willing to call Harold for me? I just don't feel up to visiting them. I'd appreciate it if you'd let him know." Helen was scheduled to spend a few days with her son at his home over the holidays. Harold lived about eighty-five miles away in the Kansas City area, but came often with his family to see his mother. Helen had recovered from her surgery months ago—and as far as I could tell she had been very much looking forward to visiting her family. "I'd probably be too much of a burden for him anyway."

It seemed her true reason for canceling was because she worried he didn't really want her—and I knew her unaccustomed insecurity was because of me. "Too much going on, too many people," I had said. By protecting myself, I had made her vulnerable.

But still I held back.

"Of course I'll call him," I said. "But I know he'll be disappointed."

I liked Harold quite well. Helen's best friend Mary Martha had once told me that Harold and his wife Becky would visit her just to chat; they always thanked her and her husband, Pat, for their continuing help and kindness to his mother. Harold was the peacemaker in the family, the one who led prayers, the one who got things going at reunions.

When I gave him the news, Harold was disappointed. It was obvious to both of us. "Please, please, please convince her to come, Esther," Harold said. "The kids are expecting her. Will you put her on the phone?"

She grinned when she heard the words from Harold and her moment of diffidence was gone. "Fine," she said. "You can't squirm out of seeing me that easily."

Helen left a few days later—and I stayed in my own bed that night. "It's not even Saturday night," Joe said, kissing me gently on the forehead and holding me tightly. "It's good to have you home tonight."

Helen had suffered so much, lost so much. But tonight she was with people she loved—not afraid to embrace life fully. I put my arms around Joe and listened to him breathe. My love for him felt as precious, and as fragile, as sunlight reflecting on ice-covered tree branches. "I truly was blessed," I thought, "in spite of my shortcomings."

CHAPTER 9
Having Fun in Life

"Everyone needs a friend to act goofy with."
ANDY ROONEY

When Helen returned from Harold's she told me about sitting around chatting, laughing, and playing games with her grandchildren and great grandchildren. I collected her stories with as much delight as a child catching candy at a Santa Claus parade.

I didn't realize at the time that she was inviting me to be on the float with her, throwing out candy myself.

But I'm being too hard on myself. I see now that Helen wanted me to share more about my own life and feelings, to trust her with these things; but it's not like I held back altogether. From the first evening we met, I opened up to her more than I had to most others even after knowing them for decades.

Since then, I had talked regularly about things important to me. We had often talked about Joe, for instance. I had told her how he could tell jokes without laughing before the punch line—something I could never do—and how he kept others engaged with his storytelling for hours, myself included. I had told her how he could not tolerate any dishonesty in others. Debts were paid on time and he expected others to do the same. "If there is no trust, there is nothing," he would say. I had told her how he helped many a needy person and never expected anything in return.

Joe's acquaintances would take advantage of him at times because of his kindhearted nature; they would borrow items and not return them promptly, ask for help and not reciprocate—things like that, but he rarely said a word.

Joe had gone to the University of Missouri in his little red Kharman Ghia with only change in his pocket and was given a room at the Baptist Student Center in exchange for taking care of the place. He'd paid for tuition and books and food by building houses full time with a construction company whose owner he met at church. Then he worked four years full time at the Post Office, all the time taking courses. He later told me he could have stayed at the Post Office there and worked his way up into a supervisory position and made twice the money he was making as a teacher. But his heart was in teaching. Money was never that important to Joe. I imagine very few young people who are determined to go to college, actually apply, are accepted, enroll, and go—all without knowing where their financial support will come from. Faith in God is the only answer I come up with. So it took him ten years to finish college. He was seven years older than I was, but we both began teaching in 1967.

His father died in 1970 while he was renting a big farming operation. That was Joe's dream—to farm. But he now had a college education and a good job. His younger brother Pete also wanted to farm, but he did not have the education and job opportunities that Joe had. It was only right, Joe thought, that his brother continue to farm the land. I'm sure the family never realized how torn Joe was in giving up that farming opportunity. He did the next best thing: He figured out a way to have his own farm, even if it meant working his whole life for it.

I had told Helen all that—and also, in not so many words, how much I loved this dear man I had been married to for nearly thirty years.

What I hadn't told her were the things I hadn't even admitted to myself: I didn't tell her about the changes in Joe over the past two years. I didn't tell anyone.

I didn't know back then that even pain could be turned into candy.

"Do you think I should join the quilting group at my church?" I asked Helen when the conversation about her Christmas frivolities came to a lull. We were packing up the decorations for the cards and calling it a night.

"I don't see why not. It would be good for you to expand your horizons beyond reading and writing and taking care of an old lady," Helen said with a wink as I stood up to carry the box of craft supplies to the other room. "And I think you'll enjoy it."

"I've been praying for a way to reach out to more people," I said. That's one thing I learned from Helen—life is about serving others.

"This would be a wonderful way to do that," Helen said.

"Yes, soon after the holidays—maybe February or March—I'll join," I said. "I should have more time then."

The next day, though, my GED teaching partner Kathy called to see if we could switch days. I usually taught Tuesdays, Thursdays, and Fridays. She wanted to teach Thursdays instead of Wednesdays. I happily agreed. Thursday—quilting day—was now open for me. The change in schedule seemed like an affirmation from God, so I began my quilting experience, just like that, on that very Thursday. The members of the group were in their 60's, 70's, and 80's—and they all became good friends of mine. Two of the members were neighbors within a block of us—Lois and Marlyn—and they and their families were also good friends of Joe.

From then on, the first thing Helen asked me when I arrived Thursday evenings was, "How did the quilting go?" I would relate some story about one of the women or some new fact about quilting. Helen seemed to live the excitement vicariously through me, so my joining the class served a dual purpose.

Of course, Helen seemed to enjoy my stories about teaching GED classes as well. She laughed at the antics of Janice, for instance—a friend of one of my adult students. Janice had the gift of generosity. Just before Christmas she bought two large stuffed animals. After she paid for them, she looked for a likely recipient. She spotted two kids, stopped their mother, and said, "You have wonderful children. May I give them each a gift?" With permission, she placed the animals in the kids' arms and walked away with nothing but their enthusiastic thank-yous playing in her head.

Another time, Janice gave her friend an outlandish present. Cackling, she walked into the friend's place of business and presented her with a gigantic stuffed moose.

"Can you believe she spent $150 on such a frivolous gift?" I said to Helen, laughing.

"Sure I can. Spending $150 on a microwave or some other appliance would not have lifted spirits as much. People complained when Mary of Bethany poured expensive perfume on Jesus' feet before his crucifixion. Many of the self-righteous said the money should have been used to feed the poor. Do you remember Jesus' reply?" Helen asked.

Her question did not need an answer. We both knew the woman had done a good thing.

"Land crabs found in Cuba can run faster than a horse," I said one day shortly after Christmas as we were poring over cookbooks, looking for the perfect crab cake recipe.

Helen laughed. "How do you know this kind of stuff?" she asked.

Whenever things got a little dull, I would drop interesting facts. "Bald eagles are larger at age two than when fully mature," or "Red kangaroos can hear a rainstorm twenty miles away," or "Wasps sleep with their legs hanging loose and their jaws jammed into the soft stems of plants." Helen's eyes would always light up in surprise at my interjections.

"Oh, I've been collecting facts since I was in grade school," I said rather apologetically. "I am reluctant to tell others about it—they'd think me strange."

"You're not strange," Helen said. "No one is strange who is doing something she loves. Lots of people collect things. You collect facts. It's a great hobby. I happen to collect teacups." It was a collection to be proud of; most were antiques from Germany.

"And cookbooks," I added. She had an entire shelf full of all the best— including my own cousin's cookbook, *Mary Ada's Family Favorites*. Helen loved Mary Ada's human interest stories interspersed with her recipes.

"Yes, cookbooks," Helen said, "which are very convenient for times like this." She triumphantly pointed out a recipe that looked ideal for our occasion—the visit of my brother Glen, who likes to travel in search of Indian artifacts. He was stopping by to spend the day.

"I just wanted him to stop by and meet you." I had told her. "We don't need to go all out. He'll probably be here just an hour or so."

But Helen had an answer. "We won't be going all out. We're staying in." I could not help but chuckle again.

"So, Glen," Helen said, as the three of us sat in our cozy chairs surrounded by plants and photos of every description, with a glass of lemonade in our hands, "what is it that you do? Your sister was trying to explain it, but it went over my head."

"I am working on resolving the paradoxical aspects of quantum mechanics and relativity," he answered.

"You lost me there," Helen said.

I stepped in. "All you really need to know is that Glen gave up a lucrative career as a research chemist to do private research."

Helen nodded approvingly. "Many will not understand how someone could give up financial freedom and comfort for a dream. But I'm glad you are doing what you like. We have to do what we like, or we will never truly live. We all need dreams or we die. Many people are walking around who are dead and do not know it."

"You are a wise woman," Glen said.

Helen's daughter, Lillie, regularly brought a copy of *Hale Horizons*, a local rural newspaper, for Helen to read. Nancy Schnare's column, "Nancy's Notes." I often read articles aloud, and Helen would offer a running commentary.

One column titled "Life Is Too Short to Eat Rice Cakes" included fourteen "Life is too short to..." lines. These were Helen's favorites. "Life is too short to wear anything uncomfortable for any length of time"—and Helen would ask, kicking her practical shoes together, "Does that mean I have to give up my heels?"

"Life is too short to not laugh at yourself"—and Helen would add, "Might as well. Everyone else is."

"Life is too short to worry much about what other people think"—and Helen would quip, "Other people think?"

Nancy was our local Erma Bombeck and Barbara Johnson wrapped up in one. Helen was, also—much to the surprise of others who came into contact with her for the first time. She may have looked like an old lady in curlers, but she could get more of a rise out of folks than any young comedian.

Helen's fun-loving spirit came out in all sorts of ways. Once the cousins gathered at Helen's daughter Thelma's in Branson, and Helen, overwhelmed by the number of people, joked, "You think we'll have enough food? Maybe we ought to cook up that dead coon I saw on the side of the road."

Everyone had a good laugh, but the joke didn't end there. Helen's granddaughter, Jeannie, at the next get-together, pretended to fix a dead bird for dinner. "I didn't want it to go to waste there on the side of the road, Grandma," she said. The stories multiplied year by year. Thelma even bought a book called *How to Prepare Road Kill*. Helen's nephew Junior gave Helen a T-shirt that said "Road Kill—You Kill 'Em, We Grill 'Em."

"I had to get this for my favorite aunt," he said.

"Don't smirk about that, son," Helen said. "I'd be your favorite aunt even if I weren't your only one." With that she gave him a saucy wink.

People don't look much to the Bible for humor, but when you think about it, some of the concepts are rather absurd: The writer of Proverbs compares a man lacking self-control to a city with broken-down walls. He also says honoring a fool is like tying a stone in a sling. The prostitute is a deep pit who reduces one to a loaf of bread. Or, a beautiful woman who shows no discretion is like a gold ring in a pig's snout.

Humor can be found anywhere.

Even in hidden places. Thinking of Rose, a mutual acquaintance, brought smiles to our faces, just imagining her and her friend. Rose, a handicapped woman with breathing and mobility problems who was confined to her home, gives a wonderful gift regularly to her friend, Ruby. In 1996 Ruby had a stroke and as a result can only say a mumbling, "Yes." When she becomes discouraged, she calls Rose and listens to her funny stories. What a gift, being able to carry on a one-way conversation, just for her friend—like a stand-up comic—or in this case, a sit-down comic.

Humor is a blessed gift. As Andy Rooney has said, "Everyone needs a friend to act goofy with." Helen was definitely a friend I could act goofy with, and, just like the old cliché says, it was medicine for the soul.

At 92, Helen was still having fun.

That joy would shine in her eyes.

She made it shine in mine in the years to come in a way I never would have imagined.

Helen and Esther

Joe

Helen and Aswald Raasch.
Their wedding picture.

Helen

Esther and Joe Dodgen,
wedding picture

Parents. Arthur and Myrtle Carls.

Helen's family. Louise Fecher in front. Left to right, Thelma Valbracht, Helen, Lillie Lou Audsley, Harold Raasch.

Esther's siblings. Ruth Werrries, Esther, Glen Carls, David Carls

Grandma and Grandpa Hendricker. Matilda and Henry.

CHAPTER 10
The Gift of Kindness

"The truest greatness lies in being kind."
ELLA WHEELER WILCOX

A beautiful flower was once discovered on the edge of the crater of Vesuvius, the volcano in Italy. In a little hollow in the lava, ashes and dust had settled, and when rain fell there was rich soil ready. A bird or perhaps the wind had borne a seed and dropped it into this bit of garden on the crater's lip, and a sweet flower grew. No wonder an observer was moved by a glimpse of beauty in such a desolate place. As we journey through life, we often come upon discouraged lives; but there is hardly anyone who will not respond to some genuine thoughtfulness or kindness.

People were kind to Helen after the death of her husband. Now she could help other potential flowers bloom.

Early spring was the time to begin gardening at Helen's house. Oh, the coming of spring! We felt the fresh air rustling through our hair and detected the fragrance of honeysuckle.

Helen loved to garden, but was less able these days, so she directed me from the porch. Most of her gardening now was on the porch. All last summer I had been there amidst the blossoming array of flowers, but I hadn't noticed that the flowers were not chosen at random. Helen had a method to the selection as to color, size, texture, and blooming time. The arrangement was part of the therapy that flowers give. They spoke of God's majesty.

While we were discussing the types and colors of petunias and snapdragons Helen wanted this year, Helen's neighbor Barb came over to ask if she could borrow a flowerpot.

"Of course you may," Helen said. "These old legs won't get me down there, so why don't you go down to the basement yourself and pick out what you want."

Barb moseyed on down, found the perfect pot, and then sat down on the front porch—and complained. Her back ached, her kids were too busy to visit, and she had paint peeling off her bathroom wall.

I continued to rake the nearby flower bed, but Helen turned her attention to her friend. Helen was most certainly listening to Barb, but she never once offered false sympathy. To tell you the truth, I can't remember that she said anything at all. Helen didn't confront Barb's negativity or offer platitudes to try to make things look better. She just listened. But the magic still happened. Barb's complaints disappeared. She still had her problems, but after talking them over with Helen she had a better outlook. It wasn't so much what Helen said; it was how she made Barb feel.

Of course, it didn't always go that smoothly. One time I had overheard Helen tell Barb that she didn't need to be on welfare, that she needed to get a job. That hadn't gone over so well. But it was probably the truth. And Barb was back today for more of Helen's medicine.

Helping neighbors was always simple for Helen. Whether it was taking a bowl of applesauce to Pearl or preparing a whole meal following the death of someone's loved one or listening to the complaints of her friend, Helen always took the time to do whatever she could. It did not matter who it was or what they wanted. In her younger days she often took food to help anyone she could. She usually had the family who had lost a loved one come to her house and stay for the evening meal after a funeral. "At times like that, it is important for everyone in the family to be together," Helen told me.

Pearl wandered over about the same time Barb was walking away. "No one pays any attention to me," she complained to the therapist on the porch.

I had been to Pearl's house many times since my first visit in August, delivering applesauce and oatmeal cookies and other goodies Helen sent her way—and had even started to enjoy her company more; but whenever Helen was present, Pearl seemed to forget I was there. With that in mind, I found her comment rather ironic.

"Pearly, you need to understand that others have problems," Helen said, reaching over to pour her friend a glass of lemonade. "You don't make it easy for them." This time Helen didn't tolerate the complaining, and I was surprised to hear her be so tough on her friend. Helen knew Pearl needed people who would take an interest in her. Helen herself had told me much of her sad story.

"As a young girl, Pearly was taken from her home and put to work with another family—not a loving family, just a family that wanted a worker. She learned early in life what hard, cruel work was. This had a life-long effect on her."

Helen knew from her own experience that the difficulties and joys we go through affect us throughout our lives. For example, during the drought in the mid-thirties, corn was just nubbins and the dust was six inches thick in places. There was nothing to sell. You learned to save for the "rainy" day—in this case, the "dry" day. After that, it was hard not to scrimp and save.

"Pearly's childhood difficulties probably explain why in her later years she had few friends and often alienated those who tried to help and befriend her," Helen had told me. Everyone knew Pearl. She was unabashed in her flagrant outcries. "As an adult, Pearl had a botched lymph node operation and now had difficulty using her right arm. She certainly has had a tough life. I, for one, intend to give her as much grace as possible. Heaven knows she needs it."

But today Helen didn't appear to be showing any mercy—when seconds before she had been extremely forgiving to a less needy recipient.

"My niece doesn't visit anymore," Pearl whined on, as if Helen hadn't said anything. "Why doesn't she come? It hurts my feelings."

"Your niece's feelings have also been hurt," Helen said. Helen talked to her niece from time to time and knew the other side of the story. "People who have hurt our feelings often have done so because someone has hurt their feelings."

"Are you trying to say that this is my fault?"

"I'm saying that you need to be more considerate of her," Helen said as she handed Pearl a cookie. "Pearly, I'm trying to help you get your niece back. If you're going to ask me a question, I'm going to give you the answer."

Pearl sulked, but I could tell she took the advice in. Did she follow up? I do not know. Apparently Helen knew her friends well enough to know when to push.

It wasn't just flowers growing in this garden.

It rarely is.

My mind flitted back to days in another garden, back when I was a child.

My mother was there, patiently answering all my questions and tolerating my mistakes. "Is this a weed or a plant, Mom?" I would ask time and time again. I wanted to be good at this task. Life in our household revolved around gardening. I remember many times sitting on the benches of our grape vine arbor—Mom called it a "pergola"—outside our back door while we snipped beans or hulled peas.

My siblings and I grew up loving vegetables and I wanted to be able to provide as many of our favorites as my mother did from her immaculate garden. I asked question after question, "Why doesn't it grow faster? Where do all these weeds come from?" Mom didn't ever seem to get tired of my questions. In fact, I don't remember a harsh word from her lips ever—whether it was in the garden or around the stove where she taught me to cook or over the table where my sister and I worked on our 4-H sewing projects. Mom would pull up weeds beside me, calmly dump out a poorly made broth and start again, or patiently take out seams so we could redo them. I'm sure she must have grown impatient at times, but I don't have any recollection of it.

A memory suddenly flooded my mind, back to when Mom taught me how to make flower arrangements for my 4-H project. "Not so many, Esther. Fewer is better," came her patient tones. "You want to make sure there are an odd number of flowers. Try a little foliage here and a bud there." She would tend her own arrangements daily—cutting back and rearranging.

Mom always had a big vegetable garden like her mother's, but she also always had flowers. Her flower garden was a nature paradise. Hollyhocks, petunias, poppies, nasturtiums, dahlias, peonies, tulips, roses. Little German paths that wound throughout her flower garden made it more than a flower garden. I remember walking down the little paths with her and feeling it was more like a flower experience than a mere garden. The larkspurs, the bachelor buttons, the rose moss were all arranged to bring out the best in each, with color combinations that inspired. Flowers improved her little corner of the world. She had flowers in the garden, flowers around the house, flowers in beds in the yard, and always, it seemed, three or four arrangements in the house when her flowers were in bloom. She taught us to see the beauty of nature—and her lessons took hold with us. My sister and I both love flowers.

I smiled. Mom would have been proud to see me now—working away in a garden without muddling it up at all.

I have never been one to get too emotional, but I *do* know what a lump in the throat feels like.

I got to know many of Helen's neighbors. Helen always had time for anyone who stopped by. Even though she could not go to them, they found a way to come to her. In Helen's eyes each one was special.

Martha—not to be confused with Mary Martha—was a woman of simple means who was often ignored by others, but Helen took an interest in her. She treated her with dignity and gave advice disguised in little anecdotes. Because of this Martha's life simply blossomed. She complained less and began treating others like Helen treated her.

One unseasonably warm evening, as we were peeling apples on the porch, with the breeze whispering between our rocking chairs, Helen looked over at her neighbor's apartment building, the former doctor's hospital. "Do you think Martha has locked herself out of her apartment?" Helen asked.

Martha was clearly struggling to get into her house.

"I'll go over and see if I can help," I said.

When I approached, I noticed that Martha had a table knife wedged between the door and frame.

"Hi, Martha," I said. "Did you lock yourself out again?"

Martha looked at me and shrugged. "Guess so."

"Did you call the landlord?"

"Yeah. He's gone for the weekend."

"Don't worry," I said, thinking about Helen watching from across the driveway. "We'll figure something out." We checked the windows. They seemed to be tightly locked with screens in place.

Finally we walked back to Helen's. "At least you know your place is locked up well," I offered as we sat down on the porch—which didn't help Martha's mood much.

"Why don't you call the police?" Helen suggested. "They'll know what to do."

We spent the next half-hour chatting, with Martha's agitation slowly receding, as we waited for an officer to be dispatched, and then we all strolled over to Martha's house together when he arrived. He pried the screen off a lower window and found the window unlocked. Then Christy, a neighbor girl, crawled inside and unlocked the door from inside.

"That'a girl, Christy," Helen said. Christy was one of Helen's life students. The little girl often came over to visit her old friend; and, even though there was at least eighty years difference in age, Helen and Christy understood each other. They acted like two ladies at a card party.

"How beautiful," I thought, "it was simply a policeman, a young girl, an old woman, a middle-aged woman, and a woman in need—all coming together. The ordinary again turned into extraordinary."

The excitement of the evening was over, and Helen and I strolled back to the porch, and then finished peeling the apples. Helen was busy talking about something else—the importance of prompt service by the police, I think—but I was thinking about how many people knew and loved my patient. This incident was just one of many illustrations of how Helen was an important part of the tapestry of the neighborhood. Her gift to her neighbors at this stage in her life was the time she took for them.

"Jesus was very clear about caring for people, regardless of their station in life," Helen said when I complimented her on her neighborly ways. "'I tell you the truth; whatever you did for one of the least of these brothers of mine, you did for me.' That's what He said."

I nodded. Helen had more right than anyone I knew to quote that passage.

"Do you remember Jesus' comments about the faithfulness of the disciple who gave a cup of cold water to one of God's little ones?" she continued.

"Yes," I said, "and that's what you do. Think of Margaret and all the things you did for each other. Or Eddie—just having time to say "hi" as he stopped by with his dog. You brightened his day."

I suppose I should have gone on. I should have told her how she had given me so much more than a cup of water. She had opened my eyes to see my world in an entirely new way.

CHAPTER 11
Using One's Gifts in Service

"We send out our energies in the service of others and there comes back to us that which becomes food for our souls."
RALPH W. SOCKMAN

It was hard to convince myself to give up the smell of lilac bushes and the feel of warm wind in my hair that lovely spring day, but Helen had the local newspaper, *The Carrollton Democrat*, spread out on the table in her small, cluttered kitchen. "Did you see the picture of Brian and Kelsey with their duct-taped outfits standing beside their duct-taped car ready to go to the prom?" she asked me as soon as I put down my bag and entered the kitchen.

Brian and Kelsey were two local high school students. Brian had dreamed for the past two years of entering the contest, and this year he found a willing partner in Kelsey.

"They sure went to a lot of work, didn't they?" I said, leaning over the paper to read it.

"Don't they look sharp?" Helen was preparing a plate of veggies to bring outside.

I could not help but be amused. "I would have thought that a ninety-one year old woman would think it a lot of nonsense going to those extremes for something so frivolous."

"I may be old, but I know a good thing when I see it," Helen said. As if to prove her point, she popped a cherry tomato in her mouth and munched it thoughtfully as she looked at the picture over my shoulder. "They showed a lot of spunk. Kelsey and her mom put in over fifty hours on the dress and Brian put in more than that on his outfit and the car."

I pulled up the paper and read some more about the competitors. Helen picked up a magazine and started to move to the door. "They've certainly thrown themselves into this, haven't they?" I said, following her. "It would sure be nice if they won the nationwide contest."

"Winning is not that important," Helen said. I moved in front of her to hold the door open and she bustled through. "It is their dedication and camaraderie that matter. It is what you become because of the experience that counts." She set down her tray on the table and prepared to settle in a chair.

"They're great kids," I said. I could see why Helen liked the story of Brian and Kelsey so much—their efforts were above average. "They remind me of your grandkids."

Helen glanced up at a photograph of her grandchildren just inside the doorway and smiled at it—children who were above average in many ways. No wonder Helen believed so much in the next generation. "Children are God's ministers to us. There is no doubt about it. They preach to us hope in the future."

"Parents usually get that mixed up," I said, laughing. "Parents do most of the preaching as far as I can tell." I put down the paper and sat down in the chair opposite Helen.

"Well, kids do need discipline, that's for sure," Helen said. She moved forward into her "preaching" pose. "But parents need to remember to say something nice before they reprimand. What the next generation will value most is the evidence of who we were and how they saw us live our lives. In the end, it's the family stories of life that will have worth, not the material possessions."

This wise woman knew a lot about gardening, but she also knew something about relationships. She knew that accomplishments don't mean much without relationships. "It's not just the harvest. It's the tilling too. Why not buy a fishing pole and take the kids fishing once in a while. Invite the cousins over for pony rides and overnights." She knew that the time to cultivate is when you see no weeds. "It saves so much time later in the season. The time to discipline is before wrong thoughts have emerged above the surface into deeds. The time to teach love is before hate has taken root. The time to teach giving is before permissiveness has sprouted."

Perhaps this insight would have meant more to me if I had had children.

As it was, I simply nodded my head as the wisdom slipped in one ear and out the other. Now that she's gone, I realize how much of her wisdom I actually retained—and how much more I needed it than I thought I did.

"The world needs more people like you, Helen," I said as I stood up to stretch.

"Oh, there are plenty of good people—young and old," she replied, munching on cucumbers. "There always has been and there always will be. We just need to open our eyes to see them." She set down the article she had been holding ever since she got to the porch, apparently accepting the fact that no reading would be done on this evening. "Think of your neighbor Lois the seamstress," Helen said. "She is in her eighties and still teaches Sunday school."

"She has a long way to go, though, to catch up with her mother who taught until the age of ninety-eight."

"True. But an inspiration, nonetheless. This past summer she was the leader of the first and second grade Bible school class."

"Yes, she is wonderful," I agreed. "I consider her a mentor, someone I can call on when I need advice."

"But it's not just the elderly. Think of that miracle baby," she said.

One evening last week, I had noticed the local paper was plopped down on Helen's bed. It was folded to the picture of Diana and Jacob and their five-month-old baby, Clara Frances. They were home from the hospital. "I know them. Do you?" I'd asked.

"Oh! It's an amazing story," Helen had said. "The baby weighed only one pound and one ounce at birth and now weighs five pounds and nine ounces!"

The article described the couple's struggles and their faith in God to sustain them during this very difficult time. Helen talked about this story days later, keeping the picture and article lying around. She was thinking about and praying for that "miracle baby."

"That little one teaches us a lot about perseverance," I now said, covering up the vegetable platter with the newspaper so bugs wouldn't get near it.

"And there's Beverly who always seems to know when someone is discouraged and sends an encouraging card or gift," Helen said. She was now leaning back in her seat, preacher pose forgotten. "I still have to chuckle when I look at that funny card I got from her when I was in the hospital."

Our list went on and on. Jeff, my pastor, loved to cook and had the gift of hospitality. You can imagine the opportunities he availed himself of in serving others. His broccoli and cheese soup and fried catfish were the best. He would prepare complete meals for special occasions at church, including a full course meal for the Ladies Appreciation Banquet, served by the men. This past spring his menu included a choice of raspberry or strawberry soup, a choice of Caesar or tossed salad, roast pork loin, roasted potatoes, broccoli-rice casserole, and crème brûlée. The tables were beautifully decorated. He even had table favors and door prizes.

Dale is another who seemed to always be doing something for someone. He devoted hours to preparing special wooden craft projects for each department in Bible school, providing all the necessary materials and instructions. The teachers loved his help. Soon after the end of Bible school he would begin making plans for the following year.

Mary, a poor woman from my church who had gone through more trials and tribulations than anyone I knew, had a genuine smile that was her gift to everyone. I saw her at church every Sunday. All it took was her smile to boost my spirits.

Frances, my dear friend, quietly inspired behind the scenes with her loving, gentle manner. Nothing spectacular. Just an ordinary person taking the opportunity to brighten her little corner of the world.

Joe was a man who put others before himself, a true example of Christ-likeness.

My mother. Yes, my mother—in whom I spent so many years disappointed—suddenly came to mind as kindness incarnate. I remembered her preoccupation with giving flower arrangements away to nearly everyone with whom she came into contact. She arranged flowers for her church for years. And she took pride in the quality of her work. If her flowers were finished blooming for the season, she used wild flowers from the roadside. I remember when we were out for a cruise checking the crops, or just driving around, my mother would spot a patch of wild roses or goldenrod, and would ask my father to stop. "That's what I need to add color to my arrangement." No matter how she did it, the arrangements turned out magnificently. She was not a speaker, nor a teacher, nor a musician; she let her flowers do the talking for her.

"You're right, Helen," I said. "The world is full of great people. Thank you for opening my eyes to it."

We fell silent for awhile. My mind was on a poem by Sam Walter Foss, "The House by the Side of the Road," which ends this way:

But I turn not away from their smiles nor their tears—

Both parts of an infinite plan—

Let me live in a house by the side of the road

And be a friend to man.

The author of the poem was walking one day along a dusty road and stopped to rest beneath a tree. Nearby was a sign that read, "Here is a spring. If thirsty, drink!" When he walked further, he saw a bench on which was painted the words: "If weary, rest on this bench!" Still further on he saw a basket of apples and a sign that read, "If hungry, eat!" He had to find out who did these nice things for strangers and passersby.

Soon Foss came to an old hut. There sat an aged couple whose faces shone with kindness. "The blessings of the day to you," said the old woman.

"I have enjoyed the blessings placed by you along the dusty road. Why are you so kind and generous?" Foss asked.

The old man replied, "There are shade trees, benches, water, and fruit aplenty, so why not share them with strangers and weary travelers? God gives us great joy as we share what we have with others!"

All the way home Foss kept thinking of a line from Homer's *Iliad*, "He was a friend of all, and lived in a house by the side of the road." The old couple's unselfishness and kindness to strangers inspired him to write the poem.

My conversation with Helen, however, revealed an even deeper, more beautiful truth. It is not just sweet old strangers who make this world a kinder place; it's the ordinary people we spend time with every day—the people who so often appear far from perfect, the people who make our lives what they are today. They all give of themselves—the only true gift. It is a language that needs no translation.

The apostle Paul exhorts us to make a careful exploration of who we are and the work we have been given, and then sink ourselves into that. When we have learned to look upon the daily course of our ordinary lives with their duties and troubles and offer them to God, we will find joy and satisfaction. We each can be extraordinary. And, whether we have our own children or not, we can make a difference to the next generation.

Like flowers, some of us bloom for only a season. Some bloom for many seasons. "But one thing is certain," Helen said. "God did not create us to squander our days in useless activity or to sit down before the work is done. Gifts are given to us, not for our own sakes, but for others: and in the end, we are also blessed."

"Can you be a friend of Jesus if you are not a friend of your neighbor?" I asked.

We both knew the answer to that question.

When I left Helen's the next morning a bobtailed cat with her three kittens sat snuggled together on one of Helen's padded chairs on the porch. The kittens were of weaning age. Perhaps the mother cat sensed this would be a good home for her kittens.

And she wasn't the only one who knew it.

CHAPTER 12
The Importance of Family Ties

"If you make children happy now, you will make them happy twenty years hence by the memory of it."
KATE DOUGLAS WIGGINS

"Get out and stay out!" a scowling neighbor lady said from the front steps of a house across the way, in clear view of Helen's front porch. It was a small, cracker box house that had new occupants every six months or so.

A disheveled man, half dressed, staggered from the house. "You'll be sorry! I can tell you that!" he yelled. He fumbled with the car door and climbed into a small red car sitting in front of the house and just sat there. As the sun set and darkness slipped onto the porch, Helen and I decided to go inside before we found out what he did next.

"This has happened before," Helen said. "It is difficult to understand how that woman can stay with a husband who is physically and emotionally abusive. I guess it's because he is kind-hearted when he is sober. I've seen him both ways."

When I left next morning, the car was still there.

I couldn't help but be thankful that my marriage didn't fluctuate so much. I suppose I sound like that man in Luke chapter 18 who prayed loudly, thanking God that he was not like the sinners around him. But I'm all too aware of my own shortcomings and family imperfections to be much like that fellow. My thankfulness was genuine—I knew my wonderful marriage was only by the grace of God.

What I didn't know was that things could change—and I ignored the hints of what lay ahead.

Joe was having chest pains again. It didn't look good.

I was frustrated. We had been to specialists in Kansas City and Columbia where he'd had MRIs and stress tests. Nothing had seemed wrong. We had considered the Mayo Clinic—a neighbor had gone there and had good results pinpointing his problem—but Joe wasn't interested and we hadn't pursued it any further.

I regretted our laxity now. He was in terrible pain, and I suspected the worst. *We should have dealt with it*, I scolded myself as I drove Joe to the hospital emergency room. It did not take the doctor long to determine that he could not help Joe. He needed to be seen by a cardiologist immediately.

I tried to breathe slowly as I dialed Louise's number with trembling fingers. I told her I would have to be away for a few days. "Joe is having chest and shoulder pains. They are taking him by ambulance to the hospital in Columbia."

"Don't you worry about a thing here. I will explain the situation to Mother. You take off all the time you want," Louise said reassuringly.

Joe had had quadruple bypass surgery two years ago. All seemed to go well. He was faithfully walking and building up his strength. Then there were shoulder pains and shortness of breath. And now these chest pains.

A stent was put in. The doctor explained the procedure and assured me that all went as well as could be expected. I stayed by his side overnight and prayed.

"I feel good," Joe had said the next day after the release was approved. "Let's go home."

Putting on a confident face, I gathered together our few belongings and we headed home.

When I returned to Helen's several days later, Josie and her man across the street were fighting again. Helen wasn't paying them much mind, however. She was sitting on the front porch chatting with a middle-aged man named Donnie. You wouldn't think a fifty-five year old man and a ninety-year-old woman would have much in common. But I had learned to expect surprises when it came to Helen.

Helen's intuitiveness, for example, continued to surprise me. It shouldn't have, but it did.

"Good evening, Esther," Helen said when I walked up. "Glad to have you back."

She smiled and asked how things went, but that was the extent of the sympathy. She knew I wouldn't have been comfortable with more.

"You must meet Donnie," Helen said. "Donnie is a former classmate of Harold's. He lives in Georgia now but comes back regularly to check on the family farm."

Donnie stood up to greet me. "I'm glad to meet Helen's sidekick." I smiled and grew confident in his easy acceptance of me.

We all sat down, and Donnie began chatting and reminiscing with Helen about the times he and Harold had gotten into mischief when they were young. Once Harold had chopped Louise's hair almost off; another time he'd put baking soda instead of baking powder into the cake he made for his mother's club members.

"Don't forget that accident with his first car," Donnie said, shaking his head. "That takes the cake! A 1950 low-lying, shiny, dark blue, visored Fleetline Chevrolet—and he crashed it the first Saturday night he was cruising around. The car in front suddenly braked for a dog in the street. The loose gravel on the road prevented him from stopping. No damage was done, but it sure scared him."

"It must have scared his mother too," I said as I stood to pick up a straw broom from behind Helen's chair.

"She just laughed!" Donnie said, smiling at Helen. I began sweeping the steps and sidewalk while Donnie got up and walked to the other side of the porch to admire the purple clematis dangling from vines climbing a trellis on the northwest corner. They were so rich and profuse you could almost hear them growing. At the other corner, pink roses covered an arbor. "Other moms would have licked his hide," Donnie said.

"It was funny," Helen replied as she slowly got up and stood beside him. She was no young spry thing, but she did like to move around a bit—and nothing got her moving more than admiring her flowers. "Why get angry?" she said. "Those were problems easy to fix. You kids were just being kids, and there's no use making a big fuss about trifles."

"Do you remember the time you caught us smoking?" Donnie asked.

"It was no big deal. Kids need to stretch the boundaries sometimes. You were good kids. Besides, who's to know why you did what you did? It's like those neighbors over there." She nodded in the direction of the fighting couple that was nearly impossible to ignore. "If we knew the whole story, I'm sure we could sympathize," Helen said. "Little do we know what goes on in the hearts of others. There is often one more fact we do not know. If we would just start with ourselves when we judge, we wouldn't have time to get any further."

Donnie grinned and put an arm around her shoulder. "You haven't changed a bit, Mrs. Raasch." He turned to me, and I looked up from my sweeping. "Mr. and Mrs. Raasch were everybody's favorite. They were always encouraging their children's friends and cousins to visit—oh the pony and cart rides, the frog hunting, the ice skating! I miss those days. Kids would sometimes stay a week or more. One time, Harold's cousin Opal stayed for a whole month."

"I remember that," Helen said. "She stayed because of the flood." Helen completed the story for my benefit.

I leaned against a white pillar and listened. It was good to be back.

"Lillie was staying at her Aunt Lucille's across the Missouri River in Wellington, and Opal, Lucille's daughter, was staying with us. That was the time of the 1941 flood. Neither one could get back home, so they stayed a month. It was no big deal. The fun just lasted longer."

"Oh, it was a big deal," Donnie said. "Opal once told me that her Aunt Helen was more like a mother than an aunt to her. It meant a lot to her how easily you made her feel at home."

"Oh, she was just talking," Helen said as she eased herself back into her chair. "Family is family, so of course she felt at home here."

"Whatever you say, Mrs. Raasch," Donnie said good-naturedly; but he winked at me. We both knew Helen was notoriously humble.

"One of my favorite memories is of taking you kids to Leta's Store," Helen said, patting the seat beside her to call Donnie back.

Donnie's eyes got big. "Mine too!" he said. He pulled the chair around so he could straddle it from behind. "John Tatham would string up lights outside the little country store, and everyone would be there."

"Yes, maybe thirty people would show up on a warm evening to play croquet or just visit," Helen said to me. I was still leaning against the pillar holding the broom. "When the weather was too cold to be outside, the neighbors would gather there on Friday and Monday nights to play cards and visit. The men would sit around a table playing cards while the women were content to chat. We picked up new recipes, better ways to garden, and of course, the latest gossip. Friendships were strengthened and courtships were started."

"What a wonderful, laid-back way of life that was then," Donnie said, clasping his hands behind his head.

I could imagine Helen going to Leta's with her children tagging along, like a mother hen with her chicks.

"So, which one of your daughters turned out most like you?" Donnie asked Helen.

"Lillie Lou," Helen said without hesitation.

Lillie, the oldest and first daughter, was the one who organized the big family get-togethers and started family traditions, like the annual cider-making day. Lillie raised a big garden, much more than the family could use, and gave much of it away.

"What about Thelma?" Donnie asked. Thelma was Helen's middle daughter, a teacher.

"She started the yearly cousins' reunion and brought them all to her cabin in the Ozarks," Helen said. "Of course, I go, too. I can't miss out on all the fun."

"Is she still as sweet as ever?" Donnie asked.

"As ever," Helen said. "Thelma took care of her husband's Aunt Gretchen when the old woman was ill and dying."

"And she's always bringing stuff over here," I added, coming back to my chair to join them. "Helen's pantry is always stocked with Thelma's pickles, homemade breads, and jellies."

"That's just proper," Helen said. "I did the same for my mother."

"Thelma came to visit just awhile ago," I told Donnie, "bringing along her homemade jellies and breads, of course. One topic of conversation was her childhood. Thelma remembered her mother saying, 'If it doesn't work out as you've planned, try something else."

"Yep. If all attempts fail, accept the situation," Helen said.

"But that wasn't true for college," Donnie said. "When Harold went to college, you said, in a mimicking tone, 'If you start, you finish. I'm not going to meet people on the street and have to explain why you quit.'" He laughed loudly. "You scared Harold to death."

"Taking responsibility, and being honest and faithful, are all important," Helen said, holding her head up high. "I wasn't so worried about the education itself; I just wanted those kids to take responsibility for their actions. It makes no difference if you live in a palace or a shack, but it is important to keep appointments, pay debts promptly, and keep promises. Living a life that is true honors Christ and blesses others."

"I'm not disagreeing with you, Mrs. Raasch," Donnie said, holding up his hands. "And it worked. You did a great job. How's Miss Louise?"

"Louise is a good kid," Helen said about her 64-year-old daughter, attempting to pour some more lemonade in Donnie's glass.

Donnie held up his hand to stop her. "She always was," he said. "That girl did it all—good student, popular, loved butchering and digging potatoes, active in 4-H—while we were growing up."

"Yes, she always liked both outdoor and indoor work," Helen agreed.

"And she's got her mother's sense of humor and wit," I added, picking up the empty glasses and placing them on the tray. "For Helen's ninetieth birthday, Louise made a wall hanging, 'You Know You Are Old When—' here, I'll go get it." The embroidered plaque was right inside the house. I went in to get it and held it up for Donnie.

You know you're old when…

Your back goes out more than you do

You feel like the morning after when you haven't been anywhere the night before

You finally got your head together, now your body is falling apart

You finally have all the answers, but nobody asks you the questions…

Donnie read it out loud, laughing the whole time. Helen laughed too. I was glad to be a part of the fun. Louise would have been happy to see how her gift was still bringing joy to her mother. Louise and Helen laughed often together. Helen loved the kidding. She loved Louise's grandchildren, too. She liked to quote her little great-grandkids, "Oh, goody, goody, we're having corn." Or "I love your apples, Grandma." They made her feel young. She got to see them often because they were at Louise's often, and Louise lived in town, not far from Helen.

"All your girls sound like you in a way," Donnie said, standing up and stretching, making moves to leave. "You raised 'em right, old girl; you raised 'em right."

"Yeah, they're alright," Helen said. "Thank the good Lord for that. Even all these flowers here you see—it's because of those girls. I'm no longer able to plant a large array of flowers on the porch here, but my daughters insist on continuing the tradition."

"They knew how much their mother loved flowers," I added, "and they knew how much time she spends on the porch." I recalled how Louise had told me, "We could not bear to see the flowers disappear." Thelma, who lives in Branson, paid for the flowers; Louise selected and delivered them; and Lillie, the gardener, set them out. It was teamwork at its best.

After Donnie had warmly said his goodbye to Helen, he leaned over to shake my hand. "I'm impressed you came by to visit an old friend," I said. I wondered how many old classmates of one's children come back to visit their parents. Not many, I figured.

"Quit calling me old," Helen shot out. "I'm not so old I can't hear your remarks, you know."

We laughed, but then Donnie said seriously, "My coming by has more to do with Mrs. Raasch than with me. I think of the Raasches often, and this little visit was more selfish than anything."

"You come by anytime, Donnie," Helen said. "You're always welcome here."

Donnie left, but I was in the mood for some more old stories. "I love hearing about the life you gave your girls," I said, folding my hands on my lap. The warm summer breeze was blowing through our hair. The huge bright orange puffs of poppy blossoms on the west side of the porch stood in stark contrast to the darkening sky. "But what I'm really interested in is the life *you* had as a girl. I know that your family were farmers, but that's about all."

"I'll tell you all about it," Helen said, "but let me get those cookies in the oven first. I had the cookie dough made just before Donnie showed up."

CHAPTER 13
Heartaches and Hardships

"We must welcome the night.
It is the only time the stars shine."
MICHEL QUOIST

I picked up the tray with empty dishes and Helen and I rambled into the kitchen. She started the oven and began placing the dough on cookie sheets while I put the dishes away and prepared tea. "My maternal grandmother, Mary, was born in Chicago, and later moved to the German community of Hermann, Missouri, where she met and married Henry Theis," Helen began. "They moved to DeWitt—I think it was in 1891—where they bought three hundred and fifty acres of good farmland and built a two-story house."

I whistled between my teeth. "They were doing alright, weren't they?"

"Yes, they were. In the beginning. But land was cheap then. They were farmers, and since this area was known for its rich farmland, they saw this as an opportunity to make a good living for their family."

I thought about my own ancestors. They also were farmers and had heard wonderful stories about the rich farmland of West Central Illinois. They came up the Mississippi and Illinois Rivers from New Orleans. When they neared Beardstown, they saw the huge horseweeds and knew they had reached the "Promised Land." It would be good farming land. They settled near Bluff Springs.

Due to the unusual circumstances of the time, lands formerly occupied by the Kickapoo Indians were taken over by the U.S. Government by presidential proclamation and were opened up to American settlers, including my German ancestors. In Helen's area the land had belonged to the Sac and Fox Indians.

I wondered whether to make mention of the harm done by white Americans to the native Indians. I did not need to. Helen brought it up herself.

"It sure isn't right, the way the Indians were treated. Do you remember hearing about the Trail of Tears and how they were forced to move West?"

"But it is only fair to say that many Christians are now calling for repentance of the harm that white immigrants, with the blessing of the federal government, did to the Indians," I responded.

I continued probing Helen about growing up on a farm in the 1920's. "So the Dewitt area was where you grew up and learned the value of hard work."

"It wasn't all work," Helen said as she placed the cookies in the oven. "Like you used to do, my cousins and I gathered eggs, fed the chickens, played in the creek, and had fun all afternoon. These little things are some of God's greatest gifts. Take them away and nothing has much value."

It was getting a little stuffy inside, so we headed back out to our favorite place—the front porch—even though the evening was by now getting chilly, taking our books and papers with us, just in case we had time to look at them.

I set Helen's tea beside her and put a blanket over her shoulders. I then pulled another blanket over my own shoulders, ready for the rest of the story. "It couldn't have been all easy," I said. "I mean, you lived through the Depression."

"Yes, the Depression was a difficult time for the country," Helen mused as she sipped her tea, aromatic with mint. "But 1923 was the time I remember as most devastating for our family."

I recalled that was the year Calvin Coolidge suddenly became president after Harding's death on August 3. In his inaugural, he said the country had achieved "a state of contentment seldom seen before" and pledged to maintain the status quo.

"I was only thirteen at the time." She remained silent, but I said nothing. Her silence was pregnant, and I knew better than to press. I continued to sip my own tea—a traditional green tea.

"Yes, I remember 1923 well," Helen eventually said, breaking into my thoughts. We were both watching the neighbor kids playing a game of hide and seek in the moonlight as their parents sat on their own front porch, but our minds were elsewhere. "The federal government was experimenting with the

Missouri River, hoping to stabilize it by adding rock upstream at White Rock. By the way, that's how it got its name."

I mumbled some word of surprise. I did not know that fact—nor that the U.S. Government's Corps of Engineers changed the course of the Missouri River.

"Yes, their interference with nature caused the channel of the river to change and in the process shortened the river by nine miles," she told me. She paused her story for a few minutes when Jameson and Kayla came scampering over to say hello, but she didn't lose her focus and continued as though there had been no interruption when they left. "Our family lost most of that three hundred and fifty acres practically overnight," she said. I could hear the emotion in her voice, as if she were still thirteen and the events were unfolding even today. "We saw it coming, but nothing could be done. My grandmother, Mary, had to move her big house to a higher place on their land, and our family had to move ours."

It seemed odd, talking about hard times as we sat in rocking chairs in so much tranquility. The fighting couple was long gone, the busy Benton Street traffic had slowed, and the children's laughter could be heard.

"How did you manage that? How did your family move the houses?" I shivered under my blanket in the chill, but Helen showed no sign of moving indoors. She was clearly engaged with her own memories.

"Oh, we had professional movers help move Grandmother's house to another section of the land." Helen shifted in her seat, pulling the pillow that had been by her side more toward her lower back. "The family tore down the barns and later built chicken houses from the lumber. These were eventually sold, so it wasn't a complete loss. My parents later bought a house a short distance away, and we started out again."

I was amazed by the change in her tone. In a moment, she went from deep sorrow to stoic acceptance. "You don't seem to have any bitter feelings," I said. "Your parents must have tried to protect you and your younger siblings from the impact." She took a sip from her teacup, but it was empty. She set it down on the table and leaned back in her chair.

"Oh, they tried, but it was like going from rich to poor overnight." She quickly learned that one can have nothing, yet at the same time have everything needful—God, love, family.

A car drove slowly past and the driver waved to Helen—another old friend, I was sure. She waved back until the car was out of sight without letting up on her story. "We did what people always do in difficult situations. We went on with our lives and did the best we knew how. We didn't sit down and give up, and we didn't blame others."

"Did you get any help from the government?" I asked.

Helen laughed. "No. It was not exactly a time of government disaster assistance." She snuggled deeper in her blanket and sighed. "But I have so many good memories from that time, too. I can still see that one-room school across the fence from our back pasture. That was so long ago."

Kayla and Jameson were on their own porch now, chatting with their mother. One of them shrieked with glee over something. After a few moments of pleasant silence, Helen looked at her watch, and we stood up together. I folded the blankets, took the empty teacups, and followed Helen into the house. Helen took the cookies out of the oven; their warm, sweet odor permeated the room. The smell of the fresh baked cookies was reinforcing memories in both of us.

"Do you remember your first day of school?" I asked as she placed the cookies one by one on a wire rack and as I molded the dough into another batch.

"Oh, yes." Helen smiled. "I couldn't sleep the night before. My first teacher, Miss Haney, was staying in our home at the time. I was one year too young to go to school, but my mother knew I wanted to go so she asked Miss Haney if she would teach me along with the others. She agreed, and you better believe it, I was happy." Her voice was full of wonder. "Mrs. Haney loved us. She made learning fun. She started me believing I could do anything. She opened up a window of curiosity about the world." The moon went behind a small cloud, but the stars were still shining in all their glory. Helen was looking up at them through the kitchen window. "Don't you think most people can think of a special teacher who inspired them?" Helen asked.

"I know I can," I said. I thought of Glenda Brown, my first teacher of French at the U of I. We still keep in touch. Talk about inspiration. She was inspiration with a capital I. "That kind of teaching involves more than just giving facts. It's inspiring a love of learning that goes far beyond the classroom. That's the secret."

Helen stuck her finger deep in the bowl to pull out a chunk of dough. She stuck it in her mouth and laughed. "Oh, to be a child again," she said.

I took a taste myself. "Remember that feeling—being as carefree as a bird."

Helen laughed, remembering. "We used to play tag and dodge ball, had ice-skating parties, organized hay rides and wiener roasts, and swung from vines over Wakenda Creek. Made-up fun was not hard to come by." She chuckled and placed the new batch of cookies in the oven. Together we walked over to the table to wait. "One time," she said, "my classmates and I put a younger classmate, Otto, in a barrel and rolled him down a hill at school. We almost rolled him right into Wakenda Creek. Fortunately, Otto and the barrel were stopped by some bushes. I later kidded him by saying if I had let him roll into the creek, he wouldn't have needed his annual bath."

"Did you get in trouble?" I asked. We moved back outside as we waited for the batch to finish baking.

"Nah," she said, sitting on a lawn chair. "It was all in fun. Otto was laughing."

"Did you ever get into trouble as a kid?" I asked. I didn't sit down because I knew we'd be heading back to the kitchen in a few minutes.

"If I did, do you think I'd tell you? I'm not that crazy."

I laughed, waiting, but she really didn't tell. Helen had a thing about preserving her good reputation. Her best friend, Mary Martha, who lived across the street from Helen, once told me about the time Helen's yard was chosen "Yard of the Month" by the local garden club. "Helen didn't think she deserved the award, so she set about trying to earn the honor," Mary Martha had said. "She called me and asked me to help." They'd waited until dark to start potting more plants to set on the porch. Remembering the comments people made about her mother when she was out mowing weeds at ninety years of age, Helen had insisted they keep the lights out so neighbors wouldn't see what they were doing. "Only two fools like us would plant geraniums in the dark," Mary Martha had said. "We could not see what we were doing. But it sure looked good the next morning."

Now, sitting on that porch that truly did deserve Garden of the Month, in the dark again, Helen asked, "Did you ever play 'Poor Kitty'?"

"Oh, yes," I said. We both started laughing just thinking about the game. All the players sit around the room. One is appointed to be the Kitty. Kitty takes a pillow and kneels on it in front of another player and meows. The player must stroke Kitty's head and say 'Pooooor Kitty' without laughing. This is repeated three times. If Kitty succeeds in making the player laugh, the player takes Kitty's place. If not, Kitty must try another player. "I remember my sister, Ruth, and my cousin, Patty, laughing uncontrollably every time Kitty meowed at them," I said. "I can still hear their laughter." Of course, that reminded me of other childhood games. "I remember going on paper trails after dark with my cousins. Did you ever do that?"

Helen shook her head.

"Oh, it was fun!" I said. "One group would start out by dropping a sheet of paper from a catalog every thirty feet or so. We'd try to pick pages that gave some clue to where we were hiding. Like an ad for bathroom accessories might mean we were behind the Dotzert's outhouse."

Helen chuckled and said, "I'll bet you didn't pick the outhouse too often, huh?"

I was laughing as I finished the story. "Fifteen minutes later, the second group would come with a flashlight, pick up the papers, and go on until the members of the first group were found. It lasted a couple of hours and was a lot of fun."

"Did you ever go snipe hunting?" she asked.

"Oh yes!" I said, laughing all the more.

"One time I went with my cousins and neighborhood kids," Helen said. "We went out in the woods with a gunny sack. The unsuspecting participants who had never been snipe hunting were left in the middle of the woods. The rest of us told them we would shoo the snipes their way and they should catch them and put them in the sack. Of course, we headed back home and left them 'holding the bag,' until they wised up and found us back at home enjoying more games without them."

"I guess all of us were left holding the bag sometime in our youth," I said. Helen got up, and we ambled back to the kitchen. I pulled the cookies from the oven and started placing them on the paper Helen was spreading on the counter.

"I remember how neighbors would often gather, eating cookies, after a hard day's work together," Helen said. During her formative years, she saw first-hand what it meant to be a good neighbor. Farmers helped each other in times of need, or simply for efficiency. Everyone did not need to own a thrashing machine. Harvesting oats, wheat, and barley was a group effort. "We would prepare a feast for the hard-working men," Helen said, "getting up early to kill the chickens, bake pies, pick green beans, and make homemade rolls. There was a lot of laughing and talking as we prepared a meal fit for a farmer."

Helen's parents were poor by today's standards—financially challenged, but not poor in spirit. They always raised a big garden, and during the growing season no visitor ever left their driveway without taking home some of the bounty from their garden.

"If the garden was not producing at the time, Mother would present our visitors with some black walnut kernels, a 'tater' from her beautiful lavender dahlias, flower slips, some Irish cobblers, or a jar of sorghum molasses or blackberry preserves," Helen continued as she dropped fresh dough onto the hot cookie tray. "Everybody was in the same boat. People gathered together and visited. Everyone helped each other. When you had apples, plums, apricots, or whatever, you shared with your neighbors," Helen told me. "You always had something the neighbors could use, and they always had something you could use. We sold eggs for a little money for sugar and flour, and raised the rest of our food."

Helen sat down at the table. I put a few cookies on a plate and brought them over. We both picked one up and started to nibble.

"I remember," Helen continued, "when corn was ten cents a bushel and wheat was thirty-five cents a bushel." She held out her cookie as she gestured. "You could sell a few fox skins, raise a little sorghum for molasses, eat wild game, deliver coal, or chop wood. You can get by on very little when it is necessary."

"You didn't have or need much money, did you?" I asked.

"People were so scared of going broke they would not buy anything, and soon they were broke anyway. Money became very scarce, and you could not even buy the things others had for sale."

Helen remembered her parents refusing to lay off a hired man during the Depression and going without things rather than allowing others to do without. The children saw first-hand the value of sticking to convictions.

"Getting rich is not the way to well-being. It takes a lot of time and can distract you from your true work. Your best bet is peace of mind," Helen said.

"'He who is kind to the poor lends to the Lord,'" I said, quoting Proverbs.

"Yes," Helen said. "And she who stays up past her bedtime feels it the next day. Are you able to finish up those cookies?"

I certainly was, so Helen slipped off to bed, choosing to focus on the future rather than the past.

CHAPTER 14
Joy is God's Love Echoing Through Us

"Contentment is one of the flowers of heaven, and if we would have it, it must be cultivated; it will not grow in us by nature."

CHARLES H. SPURGEON

The local Fourth of July celebration sponsored by the fire department always drew a large crowd in Carrollton. This little rural town of nearly 4,000 was a great place to raise kids. Its reputation was known far and wide. It had an A+ school, a designation given by the state to a select few schools. All students graduating who met other high standards for four years—like good attendance, no drug use, no discipline problems, good grade point average—had the first two years of college paid for by the state.

It's a good town. Just this year, Carrollton was one of ten cities in the U. S. designated as an all-American City by the National Civic League. Local groups had built a skateboard park, a walking trail, a new library, and refurbished the downtown area with a lot of community support.

I, however, wasn't much into parades and fireworks. I preferred to celebrate the freedom and beauty of this great country by going off to enjoy all it had to offer with just a few others.

This year the holiday fell on a Wednesday, so on the Saturday before, Joe and I took the neighbor kids—two boys and a girl—up to our farm to go fishing in the two lakes filled with catfish and crappie. It was mostly Joe's idea. He was as excited as the kids themselves, and just as rambunctious. The kids' parents, of course, seemed glad for the break: this was a rowdy bunch.

The evening before Joe and I had taken the kids out digging for worms at a friend's farm just north of town. It was a short evening followed by ice cream bars back at the house. We five dug worms for bait, laughing together at the wiggling creatures. Joe had a fancy tackle box with every imaginable lure, but worms worked best with catfish—and kids.

I doubt the kids slept much that night. They were all wired up when we picked them up Saturday afternoon.

"This is for you," Joe said, handing a long, red Calypso Seahawk rod to the oldest boy, aged seven, once we arrived at the pond.

"I want one, I want one," the other two called—and Joe didn't disappoint them. He had a fishing pole for each of them, which went over well because none of them had been fishing before. Learning the value of sharing would have to be another day.

We sat by the lake in the late afternoon sun, celebrating each other's catches, as Joe captivated the kids with stories. They watched his every move with as much admiration as would a golden retriever eyeing a piece of steak—and when he pulled in a giant catfish, they squealed with delight, not at all begrudging him the biggest catch of the day.

Dusk was nearing and we heard coyotes howling in the distance. It was a little eerie—we were out in the boondocks, fifteen miles from town—but all felt safe with Joe. Still, it was getting too dark to fish, and Joe started gathering up the supplies and putting the fish—we got six big ones—on ice. "Let's pack this up," he said.

"Already," they complained. Three hours had flown by far too quickly.

"What?" Joe feigned. "You don't want hotdogs and marshmallows?"

The cheering drowned out the yowling of the coyotes, and everyone turned their attention toward the fire.

As the darkness fell softly around us and faces turned red in the glow of the fire, I couldn't take my eyes off Joe. He was busy wiping ashes off fallen wieners and toasting marshmallows to a golden treat, joking and carrying on all the while. I was more comfortable with this man I had known for thirty-some years than with anyone else in the world; and yet suddenly he seemed a stranger. The familiar became startling. When I looked at Joe it was like looking at a poem. Not at the words, but at the beauty the words evoked.

Back at the house, Joe cleaned the fish—and the kids "eww"ed appropriately as they poked the scales and eyeballs on the side of the newspaper. I sat down at the table and watched with delight, while sipping iced tea with lemon. Joe always cleaned the fish we caught—and the turkeys and deer, the rabbits and squirrels. I never had to do that. I prepared the meat, but he cleaned it all.

When we returned the kids to their parents an hour later, dirty and happy, each with a large smelly parcel in their hands, they were almost asleep. Mom and Dad gushed as they pulled their kids into the house: "Thank you so much," they said. "We owe you big time!"

We just smiled. They didn't owe us a thing. We owed them.

When the Fourth of July came, I was at Helen's. Joe and I had already had our celebration of the holiday. Since Helen had difficulty walking, it was easier for her to watch the fireworks from the front porch where the view was good and the noise was muted, and so we settled in at our favorite place to be.

"There's Eddie walking his adopted dog, Ben Little Bear," I said. Eddie, a retired factory worker, lived down the street. Ben Little Bear was actually another neighbor's dog, but Eddie felt sorry for it in its pen and asked if he could walk the dog. Eddie often stopped by just to say hi whenever Helen was on her porch, and the two old-timers talked with ease. I saw Eddie at the grocery store from time to time. He always asked, "How's our friend Helen doing?" Helen had something for everyone, it seemed. "Maybe he'll stop by on his way home," I said.

"He probably will," Helen said. "I usually get a crowd here on the Fourth of July."

"You've got great neighbors," I said. "Oh, by the way, I saw Flo this morning." Florence was the woman who once told me that she spotted Helen giving apples to a neighbor. It was my turn to tell on Flo. "She was picking up trash and pop cans."

Helen nodded approvingly. "That's good," Helen said. "Many people wouldn't bother about something so simple, but it certainly improves the scenery." Helen looked proudly around her neighborhood. It couldn't have been as beautiful as her country house, but what could compare to that cozy, quaint home. "I expect Flo will stop by too."

"If she does, I'll get the birthday card she gave you so she'll see you still have it out." Helen had turned 91 last month, and her numerous cards were still in a basket on her dining room table. Florence had delivered the card, and stayed to listen to the blast of laughter it roused from Helen. There was nothing quite as fun as making Helen laugh.

"That brat," Helen said, as if Flo were still a child. "Her lousy card was poking fun at my age."

"If I recall, you did the same for her on her birthday," I said sweetly.

Helen grinned.

We sat quietly, doing nothing but enjoying the evening. I thought back to a year ago when I first started helping Helen. Back then I used to keep busy even as we chatted—I would scrub the stovetop or root out spider webs hiding in corners or organize her Tupperware cupboard. I had to be working all the time, doing something "worthwhile."

Ironic that it took a woman with a stronger work ethic than mine to get me to appreciate rest.

My newfound contentedness transferred over to my home life as well. I no longer felt lost when all the work was done. And when I was working, like during the long hours I spent writing—developing this project I knew God called me to—I was no longer missing out on the joy of His companionship, of resting in His presence. Just as Helen didn't need me to do her housework, God didn't need me to work for Him. What he wanted from me was simply my love. And that kind of relationship, of course, allowed Him to do His work through me.

Perhaps this is what my mother was getting at when she regularly told me to quit working so much. She didn't want me to try to earn her respect or love; she simply wanted me to receive it.

I can see now what I couldn't see then, what I couldn't see even just a few short years ago: that my mother had a lot of love to give.

My mother would often take my sister and me for an ice cream soda at Edwards' Drug Store in Beardstown after we finished the weekly shopping and after our piano lessons. The sense of togetherness is indelibly etched on my mind. We would sit near the window, talking and laughing. The waitress would come and ask, "How many want a strawberry soda?"

My sister and I always said, "I do." I certainly had no trouble making up my mind then!

On hot, summer evenings, our dad and mom would load everyone up and take us into town to the Sealtest Ice Cream Shop for banana splits. Cars weren't air-conditioned then, and I remember our hair blowing in the wind. But we didn't care. We were on our way to have that creamy, rich ice cream that Sealtest was famous for. I think of that every time I eat a banana split.

"You're smiling," Helen said.

"Am I?" It's funny how the inside spills to the outside. "I was thinking of banana splits."

"Mmmm. That sounds good," she said. "Hey! Do we have bananas and ice cream? It would be fun to serve some up right now."

Actually, we had strawberries and blueberries too. I concocted a Fourth of July banana split—red, white, and blue. As we were enjoying this fun dessert on the porch, Eddie came by. His serving was ready and waiting for him. Flo came next. And then Barb. And Pearl. And Lucille. Helen welcomed them one by one. Mary Martha and Pat were with their grandkids in Chillicothe.

By the time the grand finale high above us indicated the end of the festivities, we were fully celebrating the blessings God had given us to enjoy in this great country.

"Good bye," folks said as they reluctantly left the front porch. "Hope you get some sleep with all that racket." People were still celebrating with personal fireworks set off in their own back yards.

The moon was shining brightly when everyone was gone and Helen and I finally left the porch ourselves. I put Helen to bed, took out the garbage, and settled in with a good book. This time it was *St. Simon's Memoir* by Eugenia Price. As I paused in my reading, I looked out the window at the moonlight burnishing the petunias and gladiolas with a lambent silver glow. As a breath of night fluttered the lovely tapestry and I looked up at God's majesty twinkling in the vast black of mystery, a shiver of awe raced up my back.

Funny though—the more I embraced the blessings, the more deeply I felt my losses.

But I did not cry. Not yet.

CHAPTER 15
Still Learning and Adapting

"If you sit down, it's over."
ONE OF HELEN'S FAVORITE SAYINGS LEARNED FROM HER MOTHER.

August was hot as usual in West-Central Missouri, but by early evening it was cool enough to sit on the porch. Helen's granddaughter Rhonda had spent an hour with us on the porch with her baby Lydia. The mood of area farmers was rising with the forecast of rain. The impending rain did not dampen our spirits. I remember liking the thunder and lightning when I was a child. I felt like God was speaking to me. But Rhonda headed out, wanting to get home before the rain set in.

"There goes Kelly, one of my GED students," I said as we watched her and her two children stroll by. "She passed her test last month. Her mother took care of the children while she went to class. She wants to be a beautician and needed her GED to get into beautician school. She'll be enrolling next month."

"That's a success story," Helen said. "She's making her dream come true."

"Working with hair is her special talent," I said. "Other students came to her asking for tips on how to do their hair to bring out their best features. She sometimes fiddles with it a little and comes out with something nice. She even gave me some ideas for my hair."

When she came closer, I stood up. "Hey, Kelly," I called. "Come here. I'd like you to meet someone."

I introduced Kelly and her kids to Helen. "I've heard a lot about you,"

Helen said. "You're good with hair. How do you think I should wear mine?"

Helen always had her hair looking nice—nothing fancy, just short and curly. Kelly suggested she might try a little more fluff on top. She noticed that I had taken her advice and had my hair cut shorter with more layering. "You look beautiful," she said, delighted.

Helen didn't neglect Kelly's kids. She chatted with them as comfortably as she would with adults. She asked about their friends, their favorite toys, and their grandparents. When they left, wanting to make it home before the rain, Helen wished Kelly the best in her new adventure in beautician school. Her kids skipped along following Kelly, like baby chicks trailing after their mother.

"I like her spunk," Helen said.

If there ever was anyone who liked spunk, it was Helen. She loved young people, and it showed.

"She reminds me of Deron Sugg," I said. Deron, a young man barely out of college, was running for state representative in the fall election of 2001. His opponent had big money backing him while Deron had to borrow money to finance his campaign.

"Yes," Helen said as she fanned herself with the newspaper. "Kelly and Deron both have big goals."

"I hope they both achieve them," I said.

"Being young, Deron does lack experience," Helen said, "but what he lacks he'll make up in determination and attitude."

"He's certainly matured since high school," I said. "He was one of my students, you know." I wiped the perspiration from my forehead and pulled up my sleeves. We weren't moving much, but the humidity was heavy. "He was as good and honest as they come."

"I believe it," she said. "It's too bad he probably won't win. I hope he knows that as long as he learns from the experience, he will be ahead in the long run, no matter what."

"Right. Even Lincoln lost many times before he became president," I said.

Helen raised her eyebrows in surprise, but then nodded. "Probably that very fact made him a better president. You know, even a farmer has setbacks. The successful one is the one who learns and adapts—tries new things."

"Yes, I've experienced that same phenomena in the classroom. Students learn by adapting lessons to their way of learning, which may not be the teacher's way," I said. "Some learn better by seeing, some by reading, some by hearing, and some by hands on experience."

"You must have seen all kinds."

"Yes. The successful teacher adapts to each student's needs," I said. "Of course, that's hard when you have thirty kids in a classroom."

"I don't know how you did it," Helen said. "I could never be a teacher."

The rain had started now and people were scurrying for cover. "Sure you could," I said. "You are a teacher. Do you see how many young people show up here on your porch to spend a little time with you?" My attitude had certainly changed from thinking classroom teaching was the only way to go. "Take Doug for example." Just the night before, Helen's grandson Doug had brought Helen back from a family get-together. They had been in the living room talking about Doug's job in Kansas City when I arrived.

"He was just dropping me off," she said.

"Right. And then he stuck around. To talk about hunting."

"He's looking forward to the upcoming deer season," Helen said. "He loves it." She shook her head. "That kid knows how to balance work and play, that's for sure."

I laughed. "Guess who he got it from!"

Helen laughed in spite of herself.

"Think of little Christy who is here with you all the time," I said. Christy lived down the street.

Helen shrugged. "I don't see—"

"And remember when your great granddaughter Melissa showed up with her grandparents."

"She had come to bring me a dress," Helen said, shaking her head. The continual light rain did not deter us. We knew the sunshine would soon be popping through the clouds.

"She came to spend time with you," I corrected. "I'm not sure if you needed the dress."

"So what. I loved every minute of her time here," Helen said, smiling.

"Same with your granddaughter Jeannie when she came from St. Louis. She talked a mile a minute, and even you couldn't keep up with her—"

"Yes, Lillie's daughter," Helen said. "She came to see me. I used to go to her place all the time." She sounded amazed. "I guess you're right. Young people do seem to hang around me. I suppose I've got my own little classroom right here."

"Speaking of those kids," I continued, on a roll now. "Are you going to the cider-making day with all of them?"

"Well, I was thinking of staying home this year..." She looked at me. "Yes, I'm going," she said, laughing. "I'm going."

Yellow leaves fell gently from the neighbor's ginkgo tree like petals from heaven forming a plush carpeting of rich yellow, gold, and orange below the gentle touch of fall. What a beautiful sight.

Helen had gone and come from making cider, and now, several weeks later, we were standing in the vestibule by the large side window.

"You know it's the largest ginkgo tree in Missouri, don't you?" Helen said. "The leaves fall in a couple of days. By morning, most of them will be on the ground."

"I bet I know a few things about Carrollton you don't know," I said, moving back to the living room to continue folding laundry.

"Oh? Like what?" Helen followed and began folding with me.

"Did you know the statue of Civil War General James Shields in St. Mary's Cemetery is the only federal statue in a private cemetery in the United States?" I asked. "He is the only man in American history to have served as a U.S. Senator from three different states—Illinois, Minnesota, and Missouri."

"I'm not sure if I knew that or not." Helen tapped her head. "So much up here, the old stuff keeps falling out my ears. I do know that Carrollton is the smallest town in the U.S. to have had an electric trolley."

"Is that the trolley on Highway 65 with flowers and shrubbery that the Garden Club keeps looking nice," I asked.

"You bet. This information could be put into a little brochure telling about Carrollton's unique features and used as a promotional tool to bring tourists to town. What do you think?" She had a dishtowel in her lap to fold, but she seemed to forget about it for a moment.

Helen had a way of exciting me with her ideas, although this time I suspected she wasn't serious—it was just a part of her playful personality. Still, I stopped folding too and pictured the scenario: "On the way into Carrollton, people could stop off to see the world's largest pecan in Brunswick and the world's largest goose in Sumner," I said. "Do you think the city council would be interested in our idea?"

"They just might be. We could get Wilma and Mary Martha to help us write up a plan." Mary Martha was always full of ideas, and Wilma was the hub of Carrollton. "Maybe Louise's son, Doug, would take pictures," Helen said.

We might have transformed the entire Midwest into a tourist district, but just then Pearl stopped in and our conversation turned from micro-business enterprises to where to get a vacuum cleaner repaired.

The next morning our minds turned another direction altogether.

I was already home from Helen's when it happened. Joe and I had finished breakfast and were thinking about our plans for the day. Joe, sitting in front of the television, called me from the kitchen. "Honey, come here. You have to see this." His voice was hushed.

I walked over to the television set and immediately felt a sense of dread creeping over me. Something was terribly wrong. When the Twin Towers burst into flames and people started jumping from the windows, Joe took my hand. "How could this happen?" I whispered. He was his usual calm self.

Our plans seemed no longer important. We stared at the TV all morning.

That evening at Helen's the dread was still upon me. Upon everyone I came into contact with. "Calamities make their way into our lives," Helen said quietly. "Most often we can buck up and go on. But some situations are just too big to ever get over. They are thorns in the flesh. I fear this is one of them."

It seemed impossible to me that Helen had anything she couldn't get over. She appeared so strong to me. But then I remembered. Louise had told me long ago, and I had completely forgotten. Helen was constantly in pain. She was always in fear of her leg giving way. It all started when she had angioplasty for heart problems and later had a triple bypass. There was seepage, bleeding—but she didn't talk about it. She hid her aches and pains. She thought she could cope or make it better. She didn't want to be a bother.

Then her leg turned black. A local doctor came to the house and said she should not have had the surgeries done; she was too old—which, of course, did not sit well with her. "Old. Who are you calling old?" she'd wanted to say. "You are no spring chicken yourself. Maybe you need better bedside manners."

Then in 1993 she fell. She and friends were walking around the square during the Fall Festival. Several kids were running. They cut between Helen and her friends, and accidentally knocked Helen down. She broke a leg, and had hip problems ever since. She was taken to the hospital in Liberty—stubborn, she wouldn't ride in an ambulance. Many roads were closed because of the flooding, so it took twice as long as normal to get there.

Seven years later she had a hip replacement, like her mother did. That was when I came into the picture. She tried to keep the pain from me. She was so kind and good-spirited, it was hard to believe she was in so much pain most of the time.

Because of unsteady legs, Helen fell from time to time. Her children made sure she had an alarm button around her neck to call for assistance. Usually Mary Martha's husband, Pat, came to help Helen get up. He would say, "Helen, what are you doing on the floor?" She would respond with something like, "It's just none of your business, Pat," or "It makes it easier to see the dirt on the floor."

"Wouldn't you like the pain in your knee and leg to go away?" I once asked.

Her answer was simple. "I know it won't ever happen, so there is no use wishing."

"How can you be so accepting of the little irritating things which lie all along the way?" I asked. "How can you be so content?"

"When things happen beyond our control, we have a choice; we can either learn to accept them, or we can make ourselves miserable as we struggle to change the unchangeable. Don't worry about the things that cannot be changed."

Helen's idea reminded me of what my Uncle Bill once said, "No matter what you do, some will like you and some will not. So you might as well accept it and get on with living. If you have peace of mind, you have it all; and if you don't, you have nothing."

Peace of mind was the last thing on our minds as we stared at the repeat replays on the television screen later that evening at Lucille's. All three of us had thought of nothing else all day. Terror and grief overcame me. And yet, even then, when I watched Helen staring compassionately and yet stoically at the horror before our eyes, I knew we would survive. Even this.

Concentration camp survivor, Corrie ten Boom, once said, "When the train goes through a tunnel and the world becomes dark, do you jump out? Of course not. You sit still and trust the engineer to get you through." And that's what we did.

Life went on. The leaves changed colors. I taught my Sunday school class and attended quilting classes. Joe's health continued to bother him; he had several mini-strokes. One left a slight paralysis on the left side of his face, hardly noticeable to outsiders. Two weeks before Thanksgiving, as usual, Joe's buddies, Gene, and his son, showed up and continued their hunting tradition.

I kept teaching GED classes and tended to Helen. The Christmas holidays arrived right on schedule. Friends kept visiting.

But hints of coming major changes were creeping up.

Tom, Helen's next door neighbor, widower to Helen's former best friend Margaret, called Helen "tight as the bark on a tree." He knew how frugal she was. But he did not know about her generosity with others—not even that he was a recipient of her secret apple delivery. Tom himself gave beautiful gifts as well. Because of a stroke, he could not swallow and had to feed himself through a tube into the stomach; but he loved to cook. So what did he do? He cooked and canned for others. He made hundreds of little pecan pies and gave to anyone who stopped by.

"Good morning!" he always said joyfully as I took out his garbage on Wednesday mornings when I left Helen's.

I was honored with more than a dessert from Tom this year. He gave me a musical chime that he made from flattened silverware. It is now hanging in my garage. Every time I hear it jingle, I think of Tom's joyous spirit in the midst of pain.

Yes, life went on, but the country was forever changed after 9-11.

I was forever changed.

When you allow yourself to feel things deeply, the sorrow is overwhelming—and so is the sweetness of life. "Those who sow in tears will reap with songs of joy."

I wondered what new lesson Helen would teach tomorrow.

CHAPTER 16
Problems Can Be Gifts

Character cannot be developed in ease and quiet.
Only through experiences of trial and suffering can the soul be
strengthened, vision cleared, and ambition inspired.
HELEN KELLER

We were out on the porch again as the first touches of spring arrived. The tulips lining Helen's front walk were in full red bloom. Feeling the carefree breeze blowing through our hair after being cooped up all winter made our spirits soar. It made us feel like we were riding in a convertible with the top down and the heat turned up. There is something about that little contact with God's beautiful outdoors that elevates a person's mood. We welcomed the spring thaw with relief and joy.

"I need to call Lee tomorrow to put the screen panel in the front door," Helen said. "I like the breeze coming through when I sit and think in the entryway when it is just too chilly to sit on the porch."

"I could do it for you," I said. "Where is your screwdriver?"

Helen shook her head. "Lee is in high school and he needs a little spending money. He can do it. I like to talk to him, too. Just might have some advice for him."

The next day when I arrived, Lee was there putting in the screen panel. I got in only on the tail end of their conversation.

"I'm working on a research paper for my history class, but I would rather be mowing lawns," Lee said as he took the glass panel out.

"Look at that," Helen said, pointing at the screen which Lee had successfully installed. "You did it." Helen knew that successfully completing a project was more powerful than any words she could say about Lee's research paper.

Lee did look at it—and grinned. "It wasn't that hard, Mrs. Raasch," he said, trying to keep the pride out of his voice. "Anyone could have done it."

"Ah, but you're the one who did," Helen said.

Helen caught my eye and I winked, joining for a moment in her guerilla ministering.

I wonder now how many times I had been the recipient of such care from Helen. I wouldn't be surprised at all if she considered my entire ministry to her as her ministry to me. But I didn't see it that way at the time—which was exactly what she intended.

"You have to see this," I said when I walked into Helen's house on the day after Mother's Day.

The thing Helen "had to see" was a Mother's Day article—"Mother's Day Miracles"—which appeared in *The Kansas City Star* and showed a large photograph of six babies lined up, sitting on a sofa.

As if the media hadn't already blown this contrived holiday out of proportion already. More than likely it was the card and gift shops that loved this day more than anyone else.

"This gem of a picture should be a prize-winner," I said, pointing to the newspaper on the table as I finished cleaning off the counter tops.

She stared at it. It *was* beautiful, even I had to admit that.

"All those babies were born following a previous miscarriage, stillbirth, or infantile death," Helen continued to read, apparently not noticing my unease. "The mothers had found one another in a prenatal loss support group. They helped one another through baby due dates, baby birthdays, and death day anniversaries. But this Mother's Day, they are celebrating." Helen stopped reading and held up a fist as if she had just won a sporting event. "All six couples had given birth in the past five months."

It got me.

I had made it through the church service where mothers were celebrated with enthusiasm and through a conversation with my sister who called and through the quiet afternoon alone with my husband—but I couldn't keep up the façade forever. I cared!

She set the newspaper down and I walked over to my reading chair.

"Esther?" Helen said gently.

After just the briefest of moments, I straightened up and pulled on a smile.

It wasn't Helen's fault. And the story really was wonderful.

Helen sat down beside me and prepared to sew. She picked up the slacks she had promised to hem for her former tenant and began pinning it. I was fumbling through her magazine clippings on the hassock, trying to cover up my face so she wouldn't see the emotion I knew I still revealed there. "I went to Pauline's in Bosworth this weekend," she said after a few minutes.

"You did?" I said, not sure if I was relieved or disappointed that she hadn't pressed me for more about my unexpected display of feelings. I pulled out the magazine I had selected and began thumbing through it. All was okay, I knew.

"Yes," Helen continued, not looking up from her sewing. "Lillie Lou took me there. Pauline wasn't feeling well and needed a visit. I couldn't stay home."

I wasn't surprised that Helen had gone to Bosworth. Lillie once told me her mother's middle name should have been "Go" because she loved to travel.

Margaret, a stylish woman with short blondish gray hair and a pleasant disposition who had lived just east of Helen with her husband Tom, had been Helen's sidekick on some of her trips. They were more than traveling companions, though; they had been like two sisters, sharing everything. When one baked a pie, she shared it. When one picked roses, she gave the other a vase full. When one read a good story, she related it to the other. Margaret died several years before I met Helen, but Helen talked about the times they sat on the porch and talked up a storm with Mary Martha.

Helen had once gone with Margaret and Tom to Texas to see the Gulf of Mexico. Her story conjured up for me a mental picture of Helen and Margaret laughing and splashing while wading in the water and picking up shells. They enjoyed the scenery and picked oranges, bringing back nine or ten bushels of oranges. "There were so many," she told me, "they filled up the trunk of the car with the overflow keeping me company in the back seat. What a wonderful fragrance. We had fun divvying them up when we got back." The oranges may have been a good excuse for going, but I knew Helen and Margaret did not need much of an excuse. They took many little excursions together.

Even at this age, Helen liked to experience life.

This time she had gone only to Bosworth, which was about a half hour drive. "Did I tell you that Pauline had been taken in by relatives on my father's side when she was a child," Helen asked. "Her parents just had too many children to take care of."

"No, you hadn't told me that," I said. I still hadn't fully gained control over my emotions, so I didn't want to say much. I sat there watching Helen sew, mesmerized by the quick-moving needle in her nimble fingers.

"Bosworth must be a little like Bluff Springs," she said, with her eyes trained on her needle. "Didn't you say you had relatives there?"

Bluff Springs has only a hundred or so inhabitants. "Yes, I have lots of relatives in the area. My cousin Jim lived there."

"The blind man you talked about celebrating the 4th of July with as a kid?"

Jim had inherited a disease that left him blind and crippled, physically unable to care for himself—even unable to learn Braille because of the condition of his hands. He died in 1983 after forty-eight years of serving God in his own magnificent way.

I nodded and tried to shake off my negative emotions to focus on the conversation at hand. "He was the sweetest person one could ever hope to meet," I said. I set my magazine down and leaned back. "He was an inspiration to a lot of people." In fact, he was a clay jar in which the treasure was stored. Jim's sister, Patty, once said, "I guess he might have been that way anyway without his handicap, but he was especially so because of it. I don't remember a time when he got angry or, if he did, it was because of some injustice done to someone else. I don't believe he ever felt sorry for himself or saw himself as a victim in any way."

"Remarkable," Helen said. She had finished half the leg of the slacks, and flipped it over to work on the other half. "I wonder how he could be so positive?"

I told Helen how his mother and father helped him. Jim was in the candy business. His dad built him a small stand to sell candy and gum to the people who came to their greenhouse for plants. After they started the market at Bluff Springs, Jim became the candy sales manager and got all the profit from the gum and candy sales.

Jim's dad helped him invest his earnings. Jim purchased a U.S. Savings Bond for each of his twenty-one nieces and nephews at their birth. Each time a niece or nephew graduated from high school, Jim gave him or her the bond, advising that they cash it, keep fifty dollars, and give the remainder to a favorite charity. He also supported a child overseas.

"He liked to kid and play guessing games with any willing partner," I said, remembering the time we played a geography game he made up, *Guess the State*. He gave clues—such as important crops, several cities, a river passing through, a neighboring state—and the others guessed what state it was.

"Jim sure seems like he was pleasant to be around," Helen said. She glanced up at me, and she had a wicked little grin on her face. I knew she was up to something, I just didn't know what.

"Oh, yes," I said. "He was always laughing and joking. He was always asking about the other person, rather than being concerned about his circumstances. People still talk about how they came to encourage him, and left being encouraged as well."

Helen nodded and dropped her voice. "If he could do that, there isn't much excuse for us, is there?"

I looked closely at Helen and saw loving concern all over her face. She hadn't been ignoring my pain at all.

Seeing that she had my attention, she began pinning the other leg of the pants and said nonchalantly, "If we are to accept our circumstances, I think we have to admit what they are. Don't you?"

I didn't say anything. I just watched Helen sew for a few minutes.

"How do we ever get over all the losses we experience?" I finally said. I stood up and went to the window. I couldn't stay in my seat anymore. "Not just me. Everyone. There is so much pain in this world."

Helen shook her head. "It's never easy. During my teens and early twenties, my best friend died from pregnancy complications shortly after her marriage. I remember how difficult it was losing her, but my life has been blessed by having loved her and from having been loved by her. She introduced me to my future husband."

Her lined face was calm, her soul totally present.

"It is like the butterfly which struggles to escape its cocoon," Helen continued. "The struggle allows it to become strong enough to fly. It will die if this struggle is not allowed, just as we will emotionally die if we have no difficulties to overcome."

We were quiet for a moment, Helen working on the pants—and me working to breathe. I was trying to put on my new understanding of my old knowledge that everyone goes through struggles in life. Lessons come when we need them in order to grow, so problems can actually be gifts. We take heart in knowing that even though we will have trouble, Jesus has overcome the world.

Helen, picking up on my mood change, began teasing me, but she was right. And it felt good that Helen was comfortable enough with me to rib me, which she often did. Her preaching *and* kidding reminded me that I wanted to join the ranks of people who handled their difficulties with grace and strength.

People like Heather Mercer.

Ms. Mercer was imprisoned one hundred and five days by the Taliban in Afghanistan. She remembered prison as "the greatest privilege and honor of my life." She got to meet with God in a way she never would have before.

Fanny Crosby, the well-known hymn writer, who was blind from six weeks of age, by a doctor's tragic mistake, believed that, "the greatest blessing the Creator ever bestowed on me was when he permitted my external vision to be closed. He consecrated me for the work He created me for." Difficulties can build inner strength. Adversity can be a friend.

Jim Lenihin looked upon his alcoholism as "the greatest gift of my life," as Teresa Rhodes McGee recalls in *Jim's Last Summer*. "What could have been a source of shame and isolation became a conduit for grace and redemption for Jim." Recovery brought him an inner peace and freedom that he had never known before.

The poet, Frances Havergal, was ill most of her life, but wrote letters of encouragement to thousands of people all over the world.

Annie Johnson Flint's teaching career was cut short by crippling arthritis, but she did not let that stop her. She spent the rest of her life writing 6,600 hymns and gospel songs.

Sometimes we take baby steps toward emotional health. That Mother's Day I took a giant leap. I still do not fully comprehend why God allows suffering; but I do accept, by faith, that God is sovereign and that he is a God of love and mercy and compassion, in the midst of suffering. He created us as free moral agents with emotions, a conscience, and an intellect to make choices for ourselves. And that, of course, causes suffering. Would we ever be able to know joy or love, if there was no suffering? But, as Helen said more than once, "A few fleas are good for a dog—gives him something to do."

Author Barbara Johnson says, "We cannot protect ourselves from trouble, but we can dance through the puddles of life with a rainbow smile, twirling the only umbrella we need—the umbrella of God's love." If I hadn't learned that Mother's Day how to look at pain head on while still laughing, I don't think I could have managed what was to come.

CHAPTER 17
Strength from Within

"Peace does not dwell in outward things, but within the soul."
FRANÇOIS DE FÉNELON

In late spring, on the first really warm day, Helen and I were sitting on the porch trying to figure out the directions for putting together a kite for Jameson and Kayla, the neighbor kids across the street. Just then, Johnny and his son, wearing straw hats and overalls, showed up at Helen's with mushrooms they had gathered in the woods. Johnny was Helen's neighbor in the country before she had moved to town.

I was glad to see them. I needed to get my mind off things. I was feeling a bit stressed out because Joe had just had another mini-stroke, this time while he was operating his new John Deere 7410 tractor with a new loader. In the process he tore up the loader and put a dent in the machinery shed. The new tractor was something he always dreamed of, made to his specifications—and he was mad.

It really was unsafe for him to drive, but he refused to give that up. Neither could he properly care for the cattle, but wouldn't give them up either. His mind was deteriorating and his personality was changing. It wasn't so bad that he needed constant care, but I could see he was making unwise decisions. He became angry at the slightest inconvenience. He began to complain more and more. He was depressed and took way too many over the counter pain medications. It seemed that all of his health problems went from bad to worse at the same time. The constant use of medicine for many years was taking its toll. It was too much for his system—for anyone's system.

I wished he would just slow down. I did not tell Helen that. I knew others recognized that he wasn't his old self. It didn't take much to see it, but no one talked to me about it and I didn't want to admit it. I pretended all was fine between us. I didn't even admit it to myself that my home life was falling apart.

And yet, even as I had been sitting there working on the kite with the kids, I was thinking about Joe. Whatever I was doing my thoughts seemed always to stray back to him, back to how much he was changing, to how much our relationship was changing. I was beginning to feel sorry for myself.

But here was Johnny, telling us that the weather was perfect for mushroom hunting; and the kids from across the street were excited about their kite. For now, at least, I could forget all my troubles.

As soon as Johnny started talking, I caught on to who he was. Helen had once told me about a time Johnny was completely broke: He had been halfway to the welfare distribution place when his pride got the best of him; he turned around and came home. Instead, he went rabbit hunting, and his wife fixed fricasseed rabbit for supper. He said it was the best meal he'd ever tasted.

"Do you remember all the fun we had finding arrowheads along the creek?" Johnny was saying now, after Helen had gushed appropriately about the mushrooms. "We still have a nice collection."

"Do you think kids today have as much fun with their high tech motorized toys and plastic houses as we did with our arrowheads?" Helen asked rhetorically.

Johnny stayed an hour or so, talking about the other good times they had enjoyed with Helen's family when the kids were young.

"Remember when you got stuck in the ditch?" he said.

I laughed. I had never heard this story before. "You're kidding! How old were you?"

Helen's face got cloudy. "We don't need to talk about that," she said.

But Johnny would not be dissuaded.

"That was only twenty or twenty-five years ago," he said. "Helen and her sister Lucille were on their way to Branson to visit Thelma. They slid off the road and had to be pulled out by a local farmer. Nobody ever heard of it until Lucille spilled the beans. Helen doesn't like to be embarrassed."

"I don't think anybody does," Helen grumbled. "And I don't see why anyone would want to embarrass somebody else."

She had a point. Helen's way of dealing with disagreement was to talk about something else. She clearly preferred that to either winning or losing an argument. She had just done the same thing with me the previous evening. Our town was abuzz about the upcoming school board election—Helen no less than anyone else. As she sat reading the paper just before bed she voiced her question about the qualification of one of the candidates. "He doesn't even have any children in school," she said.

I could see both sides of the issue. Although I did not necessarily disagree with her, I played devil's advocate to get her to support her position with facts. "I don't have children. Does that mean that I am not qualified to stand up for what is best for the kids? Does that mean that a person whose child just graduated from high school suddenly is unable to make good judgment concerning curriculum?"

Playing devil's advocate usually does not work well in the average conversation unless you make it clear from the start. It certainly did not work with Helen. I should have known better. Instead of supporting her opinion further, Helen simply said, "Let's just drop it." She wasn't upset. She just knew that sometimes it is best to talk about something else. As Helen would say, "Get out before the house burns down."

I was embarrassed—embarrassed at how arrogant I was. I had forgotten an important lesson she had taught me—it is more important to go away with a good feeling than to make a point or win an argument.

But now Johnny just laughed at Helen's embarrassment about getting stuck in the ditch.

"Do you remember what Mark Twain said?" Helen asked. "'It is better to remain silent and be thought stupid than to open your mouth and remove all doubt.'"

Johnny burst out laughing and Helen grinned.

"Sounds like something you would say, Helen," I said, laughing too.

"Twain was a clever one, wasn't he?"

And of course, Helen was just as clever in her own way, using the power of silence by simply listening.

Johnny left and I finished raking up last fall's remaining dry leaves from under the bushes beneath the porch ledge, completely distracted from my previous stress. My mind did begin to slip back to Joe's problems, but this time I stopped my own pity party.

I thought of my hero Gladys Aylward and what she went through. A learning disability caused Gladys to drop out of school in England in the early 1900s and become a parlor maid. She worked hard for long hours at low pay. In her late twenties, she read a newspaper article describing the need for missionaries in China and knew with single-minded agonizing clearness, that she had to go. She immediately applied to the China Inland Mission, but they rejected her application. By the time she finished her three year studies at the mission she would be over thirty. "Our experience tells us that students older than thirty, unless they are quite exceptional, find it extremely difficult to learn the Chinese language, even without a learning disability," the principal said.

Her deep disappointment did not discourage her, though. She opened her purse and turned it upside down. Out fell two pennies onto her Bible. She said, "O God, here's my Bible! Here's my money! Here's me! Use me, God."

She scrimped and saved until she could scrape together enough for a train ticket from England across Europe and Asia, a dangerous trip because of a war raging on the Manchurian border.

When the time came, she packed her meager necessities, including a suitcase full of food. Her bewildered friends and family saw her off at the train station. Day and night, the train pressed on into frigid Siberia, and finally after many days stopped in the dead of night in the middle of nowhere, it seemed, at the war zone. It could go no further. The soldiers got off and headed to the war. Gladys got off and headed back to the nearest station with her suitcases in hand. She nearly died walking back across the barren wasteland.

Without money, she then hitchhiked to China where she spent twenty years serving the Chinese people by opening an inn for tired, hungry mule drivers crossing desolate mountain trails. Gradually overcoming the natives' hostility, she won many to Christ, including a powerful mandarin. During the Japanese invasion of China she led one hundred homeless children to safety across enemy-held terrain.

In spite of enormous difficulties, Gladys survived. She thrived. She became one of the most noted missionaries of the twentieth century, inspiring many people—especially me.

Helen also showed the power of inner strength in another way. On one of her many trips around the United States, Helen's suitcase had somehow got left behind. Helen was not at all frazzled. With the help of a few borrowed items, she managed without the suitcase just fine. Helen would get dressed in her eclectic borrowed mix and cheerfully exclaim, "How do you like my new outfit?"

"I think Mother looked upon the experience as a challenge, and even enjoyed it," Lillie had told me.

Her tour guide, Betty, revealed to me later, "If it had to happen, I'm so glad it happened to Helen because she handled it so gracefully."

One beautiful early summer evening, Helen and I were on the porch enjoying the evening breeze and admiring the petunias and impatiens in their prime.

I pointed toward one particularly noisy car. "I know how we can help our town make enough money to pay for the new cultural arts center it is planning. The police department could station a car in your driveway and catch all the speeders."

"Yes. It would probably take only a month to raise millions." Helen laughed.

Then and there Helen picked up a phone and called the police station to report the speeding cars. Sure enough, the next day half a dozen speeders were stopped.

We were on the porch watching.

"It might not be enough to help the cultural arts center, but at least the cars will slow down," I said, venturing off the porch to pick dead leaves from the flowers on the ledge.

"Don't give up so easily," she said. "This is only the first day."

"You're such a go-getter," I said. I leaned over the porch and put my chin on my hands. "It makes me wonder what you would be like if you had full mobility." She spent a lot of time sitting, that is true, but it wasn't idle sitting. "What would be your ideal job?"

"If I couldn't be a farmer's wife?"

I smiled, admiring her deep-seated satisfaction with life, and nodded.

After a moment's reflection she said, "I'd have to say traveling salesman."

I was a little surprised at first, but after thinking about it realized that being in sales would suit Helen just fine. She loved people and liked to travel. Ms. Go could spread her warmth and love around the countryside. "Would you like being away at night, though?" I asked.

"Mine would be a day job."

"Perhaps you could sell flower seeds and bulbs to nurseries and flower shops."

"Yes! My seeds would be guaranteed to sprout or the customers would get their money back."

"That's good," I said. "People do better in business if they give the customers more. I remember my dad saying, 'If you sell someone a load of melons, put in a few extra for good measure.'" You are a slave if you do what is required. It is when you do more, that you become a free man. My mom and dad knew what that meant.

She nodded, her eyebrows furrowed. "Maybe I should look into this," she said. "There is no reason I can't start a business now. This would be fun."

Even at this age she was ready to start new things. No wonder I thought Helen was invincible.

But she wasn't.

In late June a strong gust of wind knocked over one of her flower pots on the porch, and Helen bent over to pick it up. She fell, and her life would never be the same.

CHAPTER 18
Reflections on Growing Older

"How old would you be if you didn't know how old you was?"
SATCHELL PAIGE

Helen and her good friend Wilma often joked about growing old.

"I forget everything from twelve 'til noon," Wilma said. She was a tall, slender woman who loved red. She had red drapes and red lamps. Her red clothes highlighted her silver hair. In earlier days she liked to go to flea markets and pick up red knick knacks.

"Don't worry, Hartman, your secret is safe," Helen replied. "I don't remember it anyway."

They joked constantly about growing old, but never acted their age. "It's not about being old or young," Helen would say. "It's about being alive and aware—seeking. You don't just look at the world with an open heart—but with an open mind, as well. When you did that, it's all so … interesting!"

To keep her self-respect, Helen sometimes had to exert her independence. Upon moving to town, she often would go somewhere without letting anyone know where she was going, much to the dismay of her children. "I still have a life of my own, don't I?" she would say. "Going to the farm and other places when I like helps me feel free." I was reminded of e. e. cummings' quote: "To be nobody but yourself when the whole world is trying its best night and day to make you everybody else is the hardest battle any human being will ever fight."

Of course, Helen might not have had a completely accurate picture of herself. She referred to several people her age or younger as poor old souls or old folks, not thinking of herself as that same age. And she was certainly not ready for dependent living, whether she needed it or not. Helen always said she did not want to go to a rest home or old folks home. "I may just have to put my foot down and say, 'No, you all go on. I'm okay here.'"

She considered her sister Lucille in a pitiful situation. Lucille was unable to care for herself, and her daughter was afraid to leave her alone—thought she might leave the stove burner on and burn down the house. So Lucille's daughter insisted she move closer to where she lived so she could keep an eye on her. It was hard on Lucille and she never did adjust.

"You won't see that happening to me," Helen said.

"At least there would always be someone around to talk to," Helen's daughters replied.

But Helen was firm. "Listening to someone carry on would be no picnic—repeating themselves and complaining."

Before Helen's fall, Wilma had been in care for six months after surgery for a brain tumor. Helen had visited her regularly. Helen was always good about going to visit friends, neighbors, and family when they were sick or in the nursing home. I once heard her say to a friend on the phone, "I wish there was more I could do for her." I never found out whom she was talking about, but I knew she would do what she could for anyone.

Once I went with Helen for a visit to the nursing home and they served Wilma potato soup with lima beans for lunch.

"You ever had lima beans in potato soup before?" Helen asked.

"Nope," Wilma said.

Helen looked at me. "You?"

I shook my head.

"Me neither," Helen said. "I'll bet they were off somebody's plate."

Wilma looked at them closely and said, "You're probably right." Then she laughed so hard she almost hurt herself.

"You two must really be able to count on each other after so many years of friendship," I said, just as we were getting ready to head home.

"Oh, yes. Helen knows the worst about me and still loves me," Wilma said.

"Who else but a true friend will tell you the truth while others flatter you or laugh behind your back."

"That's what you think," Helen said with a wink.

"Esther, you already know we laugh a lot. With us there was never a falling out. And nobody else ever called me Hartman. I don't know what I'd do without this old girl."

I was thinking of how I also considered Helen my friend and I had the feeling that she treasured the fact that I was her friend. I could be myself with her and even show off a little, or kid her, without offending her. After a chat with Helen my worries seemed to vanish like a forgotten dream.

"I could always trust her to say something outrageous," Wilma continued, interrupting my thoughts.

And, as if to prove her point, Helen said, "Speaking of good times, what do you say we go do some bowling in the hallway? It's the perfect width."

"Nice place," I told Helen when we were driving home, "for a nursing home." Now that Helen had seen her equally independent friend adjust to life in a home, maybe her attitude would change.

"Wilma sort of likes it there, I think," Helen said, apparently amazed.

"She always has someone to talk to." We both knew that's what mattered to Wilma most.

"She even got one of the helpers to order take-out because she didn't like the dinner menu for the other day," Helen said.

Even so, no one was ready for Helen's day to come so quickly.

It's fitting that Helen spent her last activity at the Benton Street house fussing with a pot of flowers that had blown off her porch ledge. As was her habit, she had her emergency alarm button accessible that late afternoon day in June when she fell. Still, I don't like to imagine what she must have been thinking as she lay there waiting for help to arrive.

Paramedics were assisting Helen into a chair when Louise happened to drive down Benton Street and saw the ambulance. She stayed with Helen a couple of hours and Helen seemed to be feeling fine. I came that evening and still everything seemed okay.

But the next day, Helen could not get out of bed.

"She needs to go the hospital," I told Lillie over the phone. "She doesn't want to, but I don't think she has a choice."

Lillie called the ambulance and Louise. The three of us rallied ourselves to inform their mother of the trip she would most certainly resist; but our concern was unnecessary. Helen was ready. She could hardly move. And upon examination at the hospital, we learned why: she had several cracked ribs. Serious business for a woman her age.

"Oh, don't worry. She'll get better," Wilma said to me with a grin a few days after Helen had been moved to the convalescent center. "There's no keeping that bird down." And somehow I believed her. How could a couple broken bones slow this power force down?

Even Helen talked about going home. "That house will be run down without me," she would say. "When'll those doctors let me out of here?" She thought she was in the hospital and didn't realize it was a more permanent arrangement.

"As soon as you can get up on your own," Louise or Lillie or Thelma would say. But they knew the truth. It must have agonized them. None were anxious to get Helen off her beautiful front porch, away from her comfortable home and all the memories associated with it.

"I certainly don't like it," Louise admitted when I asked her how she was doing with this, "but she'll be okay. Forty years ago Mother had to give up her home in the country after the death of my father. She coped then and continued on in triumph. She will do the same now."

It was true, I knew. Helen would be thankful in all circumstances.

Day after day, Helen waited to get strong enough to stand on her own. In reality, however, she got weaker and weaker due to inactivity as she slowly adjusted to life in the convalescent home. After a month or so, even she knew this was the best choice. She put up no fight—and it didn't take long for her to settle in. It was soon almost like home.

And so began a new chapter in both our lives.

I often went to see Helen in the convalescent home. I'd pop in and say, "Anyone here?" She'd give her customary Helen smile and say matter-of-factly, "Just me and the chickens. Come in and sit a spell. What have you been doing?"

On a day shortly after Helen's arrival at the nursing home, when I had a thousand things I thought I needed to do, I stopped by. I loved how her face lit up when I went to see her. I knew Helen treated everyone that way, but that didn't make me feel any less special. Her love was genuine. Her laughter was contagious.

As it turned out, nothing was as important as the view I caught of her son,

Harold, massaging his mother's swollen feet and legs. The nurses could have done it, but Harold wanted to. Helen beamed.

Lillie came into town from twelve miles out in the country to visit her mother almost every day. She often took roses from her garden to other people in the nursing home, always doing for others and putting them first, just like her mother had done before her.

Thelma came as often as she could, always loving and tender with her mother. Thelma was a dutiful, inspiring daughter, and she brought great joy to her mother.

Louise organized Helen's last birthday party (her 92nd) in the convalescent home. She made and decorated the cake and Lillie brought the punch. Colorful balloons and twisted streamers were hung. Granddaughter Rhonda and her baby Lydia were there. Her cousins Mildred and Grace were there, and of course Mary Martha and Wilma, plus new-found friends from the nursing home. Helen did not like to be fussed over, but she did seem to enjoy birthday parties.

It's no surprise to see how much Helen enjoyed birthday parties. Thinking back to her 91st birthday, I remembered how her kids had a big celebration in DeWitt and gave her a celebration booklet—"Do You Remember?" Helen still had it by her bed this year. In it, Helen's ten grandchildren, nineteen great-grandchildren, and four great-great- grandchildren had plenty to say about her. Several grandchildren mentioned coming down to stay during the summer, and making mud pies outside the smoke house. "We raided the garden and found lots to decorate the mud pies with," they recalled. They fondly remember going to Burger Bar, picking peaches at a nearby orchard, making funnel cakes, and doctoring-up Tony's store-bought pizza with extra sausage and cheese.

Twenty-year-old great-grandson Michael's words in the booklet sum up their feelings: "I can't begin to explain how much you mean to me. You've made my life extra special in all that you've done. Thank you for being you. I love you, Grandma."

Birthday party or not, Helen was not often left alone. Many continued to visit. Cousin Pauline and her husband Richard came every Friday without fail. Louis and Shirley, family friends from the country, were there often, as was Ronnie who came to visit his mother and never failed to stop off to see Helen. Of course, Mary Martha, folks from church, and neighbors continued to visit their old friend as well.

When I visited Helen in the convalescent center, I would often visit other patients I knew. Jenny, one particular recipient of Helen's flowers, said, "I didn't realize how wonderful it was to get flowers. The gift was so inspiring and encouraging I wish I would have done the same when I was able." That comment meant a lot to me. I now give flowers for no other reason than I want to. It's the same reason my mother gave away flowers. It's the same reason little kids give their mothers bunches of dandelions.

On Valentine's Day, Mary Martha wanted to "give dandelions" to Helen; but Helen had everything she needed or wanted. What could Mary Martha do? She finally decided to give her a little stuffed bear that sang Elvis' hit, "Love me tender, love me sweet, you have made my life complete and I love you so." She also included a little handwritten scripture passage from Proverbs: "Let love and faithfulness never leave you; bind them around your neck, write them on the tablet of your heart."

"The smile on Helen's face made me happy," Mary Martha said. "I remember Helen saying the greatest need anyone has is love. We feel it in our heart when it's there, and there is no mistaking it."

Amazing how even in the times of greatest sadness, even in a nursing home, even at a funeral, love is present, and there's no mistaking it.

Love never fails.

Perhaps it was partially for a selfish reason that so many came to see Helen. Perhaps they came because she made them feel good. One thing is sure: when they were with her, they had her complete attention. She came upon you like the rising daylight.

But most of all, we came to honor Helen.

She was like no other, yet she was like all who give of themselves to others.

We celebrated her simple, useful life. We celebrated the extra-ordinariness of an ordinary life. Didn't Jesus take the ordinary lily that grew in tens of thousands, and say of it, "Not even Solomon in all his glory was arrayed as well."

We celebrated joy.

Perhaps society has it all wrong. We honor the doer of the big deed, the giver of the big donation, the record setter, and the mountain climber working against great odds. Who knows? Maybe it's the humblest servant inspiring others who should be the most honored. Didn't Jesus say, "he who is least amongst you all—he is the greatest"?

CHAPTER 19
God Has Set Eternity in Our Hearts

"I am the resurrection and the life.
He who believes in me will live, even though he dies;
and whoever lives and believes in me will never die."
JOHN 11:25

Helen continued to fail, and at times was having hallucinations or nightmares and was incoherent, probably side effects from the pain medications. Swallowing and breathing problems grew worse. It was difficult for me to see her like this. I wanted to take her frail body into my arms and just rock the pain away. But I was helpless. I had to leave her in God's hands, sensing that time was short. Still, whenever things started to look bad, she would perk up and life went on as usual.

Even in this situation, confined to her room and up only with another's help and her walker, Helen continued to cheer me up. "How are you feeling about all of Joe's strokes?" she would ask me—even though it was she who was suffering with health issues.

"Mini-strokes," I corrected. "They are no big deal. They don't seem to be having any lasting effect. He just needs to slow down. What concerns me is his attitude."

"What do you mean?"

"You know how he cannot tolerate people not sticking to the straight and narrow?" I said.

"As he perceives it," Helen said with a small smile.

"Right," I said, glad to have someone who was tracking with me. "Well, I always saw some of this impatience with others, but had rarely felt it towards me until recently, when it began to escalate."

"Ouch. That's got to hurt."

"It does." It did. Especially when he complained about me to others. For example, my friend and neighbor Vaona mentioned the previous morning, laughing, what Joe told her about my cooking. It was not complimentary.

"Oh, he's just being a typical man," Vaona said when I grumbled.

But it bothered me. I knew he preferred richer food—he had always complimented the good cooks who made scrumptious desserts and other fat-laden foods—so that wasn't the issue. Since we had been married, I had kept a special diet for his gout, heart disease, acid reflux, rheumatoid arthritis, high triglycerides and other ailments—cooking sensibly. I tried to cut down on butter, gravies, and sweets. I was always torn between giving him what he should eat and what he wanted to eat. Yes, I knew he preferred richer foods; but it wasn't like him to complain—and certainly not to others.

Another time I heard him complain to someone that I spent too much time reading. I had never detected the slightest hint from him of my reading as being a negative thing. He liked to read, too. And he always gave me feedback on my writing. I would read, for example, while he watched TV. I wanted to be with Joe, but I didn't care for TV so much, so I would sit beside him reading. I did watch some, and got interested in the Kansas City Chiefs' games and of course the Superbowl—but mainly because he was watching. I would not have watched by myself. His complaint was irrational—and uncustomary for him. What was happening?

"It's just that I miss his easy-going nature," I told Helen now. "It seems like so long ago that we would spend evenings together in a tree stand or other special location on our farm watching deer and enjoying God's great outdoors." I remembered how quiet it was and how the little sounds brought us closer to God. It was this communion with nature and God that brought us close to one another.

"You did that just last season," Helen said. "Just about every late afternoon and evening during deer season, from the sounds of it." She laughed. "Since you didn't have me to take care of."

We smiled a little at each other. Helen must miss her old life too. She could relate to what I was saying. "Yeah," I said. "It's just that I miss that connection with him."

"He's going through a lot," Helen said. "Remember, he is in constant pain."

"Yes, and he's so sick of pain medication." In fact, he hadn't been his old self since the bypass surgery. He was complaining a lot, and not just about me.

I get why people like Barb and Pearl complain to Helen about their issues all the time. Helen somehow gets people to see beyond the frustration and to what to do about it. In my case, I just needed to love my husband no matter what. "If you love someone," the Bible says in Helen's voice, "you will be loyal to him no matter what the cost. You will always believe in him, and always stand your ground in defending him."

Joe was slowing down. His health was deteriorating. Helen knew it. Joe knew it. I knew it.

But, for all my careful preparation, I wasn't ready.

May 18, 2003, a Sunday morning, I had been working overnight as a caregiver in a group home, which I did one night a week since Helen went to a nursing home, and returned home at 7 a.m. to find Joe dead in bed.

I embraced his shoulders for a little while hardly believing this was happening. I knew I had to call an ambulance, but I could not get the words out. I fumbled for the telephone book. *What was I looking for?* My hands were shaking. My mind was a blur. Finally I found the number of the ambulance.

It took a few moments for someone to pick up the phone. I must have been expecting a quick grab and a frantic voice on the other end, because the lazy voice—"Hello, this is Kristy. What's your emergency?"—I actually heard surprised me.

I cannot remember anything else. It's a blur. I do not remember what I said.

After the paramedics were on the way, Kristy reassuringly asked, "Is there anyone you want me to notify?"

I was surprised again. Notify? "Yes," I said presently. "Marlyn …and Lois…and Dorothy. I gave her their numbers. All three were friends of ours from the time I moved to Carrollton in 1973. Actually, Joe was friends with them and their families from the time he moved to Carrollton seven years prior to our marriage.

I went to my husband, kissed him, and stayed with him—feeling my innards shaking and rattling with the strong emotions I didn't know how to release—until Dorothy, already dressed for church, arrived.

"He can't be gone," I said to my friend. My voice was quiet, but it shook. "We still have to build the house." The land had been cleared and the blueprints were almost done. Joe couldn't go without building his dream house.

"Oh, Esther," she said with love in her eyes. "I'm so sorry." She held me and comforted me.

I was still mostly mute and unmoving.

The paramedics were there in fifteen minutes. The two attendants, a man and a woman, were kind and professional-like. I showed my husband to them. The body was cold and no resuscitation attempts were made. "It was a heart attack," they said quietly. But I didn't need to be told.

I should have been there. Wasn't Joe more important than my job? Wasn't being there my responsibility—being by his side when he needed me most? I might have gotten help before he died. I might have comforted him during his last minutes. Instead, I was away doing my own thing. And it wasn't even a very enjoyable thing: I spent Joe's last evening on earth working beside a young lady coworker who was distant and unresponsive. My anger burned against her. Against myself. "Lord have mercy!" I silently called to the One person who was free from my wrath. "You are in control. Help me."

The paramedics took his body.

Soon our pastor and others from the church arrived. I had a Sunday school class to teach that morning. They worked out arrangements for my class to go in with another class and made sure I had everything I needed.

Everyone except Dorothy left. Then my best friend Saundra came. She had been going through difficulties also. She understood me. She was one I could confide in. "Why, Saundra?" I kept asking. "Why now?"

Still, when Saundra finally left, I was a mess. I didn't know what to do.

I called Hazel, Joe's sister. I knew she would notify the rest of the family.

I called my sister Ruth in Illinois. "Do you want me to come over?" Ruth asked. I knew she would do it. My sister had been the one who was there for my mom in her last years. She checked on her daily and brought homemade foods, saw that she got groceries, and took her to places she needed and wanted to go. She was always so generous with time and help. My brothers, who lived nearby, had helped too.

"No," I said. I couldn't do that to her. It was the time of spring planting. Ruth was a major part of her family's big farm operation. She took meals to the field for all the workers, went to town for parts, ran other errands, helped move machinery, and a host of other things. It was not a good time for her to be away from home. "Everything is under control," I said. "I have my church friends and my best friend Saundra."

"Are you sure?"

"Yes."

I paused.

"Are you okay, Esther?"

I wasn't. "I should have insisted on taking Joe to the Mayo Clinic," I said.

"You did everything you could, Esther," Ruth said. "Think of how many doctors you took him to in Kansas City and Columbia."

"Yes, but they couldn't seem to pinpoint the problem."

"Exactly. Even if you had gone for more tests, you could not have prolonged his life," Ruth said. "You're not God."

She was right, of course.

"He's really gone."

"He had a good life," Ruth said.

Yes, he did. He accomplished so many of his dreams.

He'd established a fund for awarding scholarships to worthy Mizzou students, anonymously, through his old church in Columbia and through the Baptist Student Center. He was so grateful for the Student Center taking him in when he started out in college without a dime in his pocket.

He had touched the lives of many students. He'd started the Carrollton Chapter of the National Young Farmers, the first one established in the state. He'd served as advisor for the group for thirty years and organized many unique educational activities. Every year he encouraged his group to attend the National Institute—from Georgia to Wyoming, to Texas, to Utah, to Pennsylvania, Indiana, California—to visit farming operations all over the country, to study and learn about new ideas in farming.

He had a farm and was continually improving it. He had a thriving, show-quality cattle operation that he started from nothing. And he was God's faithful servant for sixty years, always thankful for what God had given him.

I looked out the window at the May rain falling steadily down. I saw the buds on the pink flowering beauty bush and the white clouds breaking through the black ones. Yes, he had a good life.

Just not enough of it.

I put my face in my hands.

And I cried.

Quietly at first. But my trembling turned to shaking, and my sobs turned to wailing.

Joe was really gone.

My sister's husband, John, bless his heart, insisted that she go to me no matter what I said. Ruth drove the two hundred miles, and was at my home in Carrollton by early afternoon. She stayed until the day after the funeral. What a blessing she was. What a godsend. I didn't want to take her away from her responsibilities. But through her husband's generous and loving attitude, God was at work again.

No autopsy was performed. On the death certificate it read cause of death: atherosclerotic heart disease.

The funeral was simple, like Joe would have wanted. No eulogies. Just the simple, glorious gospel message and songs of praise.

"Amazing grace, how sweet the sound that saved a wretch like me. I once was lost but now am found. Was blind but now I see."

"He'll call me someday to my home far away, where His glory forever I'll share."

"And when I think that God His Son not sparing, sent Him to die, I scarce can take it in."

That lovely spring day of his funeral, that spoke of resurrection, many people mourning his death came and spoke to me, I knew even then I would be okay—because I felt both pain and joy.

Grief visits all who live long enough and love deeply. When we lose a loved one or when we experience any other profound loss, darkness overwhelms us for awhile. "Weeping may endure for a night, but joy cometh in the morning."

People weren't afraid to poke fun at Joe even now that he had died. Even I did. I recalled one time he and I went to a farm machinery auction, or rather planned to go. Joe saw the ad in the paper and knew the general direction from Salisbury. I had asked if he needed to get directions ahead. He didn't think so. "There will be signs along the way," he said. When we got to Salisbury, we saw no signs.

"Why don't we get directions?" I asked. "I'll ask that man over there." There was even a John Deere dealership nearby. "I'll go in and ask," I said. To no avail. I now smile at that old cliché about men not wanting to ask for directions. That was so true for my man. We drove all around and never did find the auction.

At this point, I couldn't have cared less that in his last year he had become rather ornery; now even those memories are sweet. But what mostly comes to mind are the good times we had—sitting on the pond bank with fishing poles in our hands, basking in each other's presence, knowing the other was there for life, through the good and the bad, and just thanking God for the simple things. Or little romantic outings on various trips around the U. S. where he would take time to relax and enjoy being alive.

"I'm so sorry to hear about your loss. I wish there was something I could do." It was Audrey, the distant and unresponsive young coworker of mine from the group home—and she meant it.

"You already have," I said. What she did was knock the negativity out of me. I had been judging her without even realizing it, and her kindness to me shook me out of my self-pity. How wrong I had been about her. Audrey turned out to be one of the most supportive people to me as I dealt with Joe's death. And after I found out that Audrey's husband was in jail for dealing drugs and that she was having trouble with her two sons, I appreciated her support even more.

Really, though, Audrey wasn't the only one who rallied around me. Friends and family were praying for me, regularly checking in on me, bringing me meals, helping me adjust to my new life. My quilting friends were there. *Oh God, how good you are to me!* I thought back to how convinced I was that God had a hand in leading me to that group. God's love mingled freely as these ladies comforted me. It must have been for a time like this that He drew me to that group four months ago.

I had to sell the cattle, then the machinery, and finally, six months later, the farm—I couldn't handle the farm alone, of course—and folks not only advised, but cared. They seemed to understand how painful this was for me to let go of a dream, of memories, of Joe.

And Helen, of course, was always there for me, ready to listen.

"Joe memorized 300 Bible verses when he was in the fifth grade," I said to Helen one day when I visited her in the nursing home. "I never knew that. A former classmate of his told me that at his funeral. She used to stay in from recess because she wanted to listen to him recite the verses."

"He was quite a guy," she said warmly.

He was quite a guy. I choked up and Helen waited, clucking encouragingly. This whole crying thing was getting time consuming.

Epilogue

"He who has gone, so we but cherish his memory, abides with us, more potent, nay, more present than the living one."

ANTOINE DE ST.-EXUPÉRY

And now I'm crying again. Not just because Helen, who had been so dear to me, was gone; but because I understood how much good there is in mourning the death of those we love. I'm crying today for Helen, but also for Joe. And for my unconceived children. And, most certainly, for my mother.

Sometimes it's not until years after an event that I catch the hint of truth behind it. I can be so busy, busy, busy running to achieve the abstract that I don't sit on the porch long enough to hear God's voice comforting me through his Word—and in the splendor of his work, outside, and in us.

Today though, I get it. I'm listening. I'm lounging on the porch.

"A lot of water has gone under the bridge in my life," Helen had told me a few weeks before her death, "and the world has been good to me. I hope to see a few more years of water under the bridge, but I do not have the say-so about that. I will be ready when the time comes. God will take care of that."

Helen's health had been fading. A stroke left Helen with swallowing and breathing problems and the family chose not to have a feeding tube installed, just as Helen wanted. She died peacefully amongst the quiet conversation of others in the room. Lillie was there, as she always had been. It was as if Helen were waiting for Lillie to come before she let go.

When the time came, Helen went with no complaints. She knew that death was near and was at peace with it. She did not care to change the scheme of things, since she had for the most part enjoyed every bit of life and was well satisfied. She was happy in her house by the side of the road, being a friend to all. She did not wish for more. God had it all worked out. "When it comes time to die, make sure that's all you've got left to do," Helen had once said. And that's what Helen did.

On a cool, crisp Saturday, folks had gathered, as I did, at Helen's estate auction, hoping to get a few keepsakes to remember her by. She didn't have much—she followed more along the lines of what Emily Dickinson wrote: "My friends are my estate." That was smart estate planning. The treasures I did find included a pincushion, a little basket, a letter opener, and a cup from Germany; but the real gem I discovered in one of the boxes was a four-page booklet in Helen's own handwriting. I was surprised at how much the handwriting looked like my mother's. And, in my mind's eye, I see my mother's smile, as if it were her little joke.

The four pages of loose leaf paper were tied together with bows made of white yarn and contained a hand written copy of an article from *Farm Journal*, titled, "I'm a No-Till House Keeper." It was a funny and revealing article, vintage Helen. The article concluded with, "I'd like to be buried with my work clothes and boots on. I may have to do a few chores when I get to that Big Farm in the sky."

I pull that article out of my purse and glance at it one more time.

I'm not crying anymore. I'm smiling.

About the Author

Esther graduated from Triopia High School in 1961 and the University of Illinois in 1967 where she was a teaching assistant while working on her master's degree. She spent a year studying and traveling in Europe. She received diplomas from Alliance Francaise in Paris and Laval University in Quebec. Her first teaching assignment was teaching French at Illinois Valley Community College in Oglesby, IL.

In 1973, Esther married Joe A. Dodgen, a farmer and vocational agriculture teacher, and began teaching at Carrollton High School in Carrollton, MO., with her husband She retired from teaching after 30 years and taught GED classes part time. After her husband's death in 2003 she moved to Jacksonville, IL where she had many relatives.

Esther taught Sunday school and Bible school for 30 years in Missouri. After moving to Jacksonville, she was a faithful member of Lincoln Avenue Baptist Church, led the Monday morning Ladies Bible Study Group, and taught the senior women's Sunday morning small group. She especially enjoyed reading, writing, and listening to classical music and had a special fondness for nature, animals and children. She had three published works: "Flowers Along the Path: Collected Wisdom for Your Spiritual Journey," Barbour Publishing, 2001, "Glimpses of God through the Ages: A collection of Personal Expression of Faith from the Bible to the Present," Hendrickson Publishers, 2003, and "Bouquet of Flowers: Inspiration Gathered from My Spiritual Garden," Published in 2010 by Author House.

Esther went to be with the Lord in 2010.

LaVergne, TN USA
14 March 2011
220095LV00001B/8/P